Tuscania

Moments in Time and Panoramas of Italian Art

Italo Faldi with notes and up-to-date information by Ferruccio Canali

BONECHI
edizioni il Turismo
FIRENZE - 1954

Agent for Lazio (excluding Rome):
Archidee di Claudio Tini
Località Sant'Egidio
01032 Caprarola (VT)
Tel. and fax 0761 647540

The large type face is the text by Italo Faldi, identical to the first 1981 edition (a few excerpts have been shifted elsewhere or included under other sub-titles); notes and additions by Ferruccio Canali are in smaller type face and in square brackets.

The drawings on pages 27 and 72-73 are by Virgilio Galati

The attributions of the works on pages 36, 37, 38, 39 (the *Nativity, Saint Francis* and the predella of the large altar-piece on the high altar) in the church of Santa Maria del Riposo are from a forthcoming study by Dott. Fulvio Ricci, in charge of the Art History Section of the Cataloguing Center of Cultural Assets in the Province of Viterbo, to whom we wish to present our sincere thanks for his collaboration.

© Copyright 2000 by Bonechi Edizioni 'Il Turismo' S.r.l.
Via dei Rustici, 5 - 50122 FLORENCE
Tel. +39-055 239.82.24
Fax +39-055 21.63.66
E-mail: barbara@bonechi.com
          bbonechi@dada.it
http://www.bonechi.com
All rights reserved
Printed in Italy

Revision of texts and iconographical research: Lorena Lazzari
Photographs: Archives of Bonechi Edizioni "Il Turismo" S.r.l., taken by:
          Anselmo Mancini – Tuscania
          Lorenzo Cerrina – Florence
          Claudio Tini – Caprarola
          Francesco Biganzoli – Viterbo
          Photographic Archives of the Art History Section C.C.B.C.
          Amministrazione Provinciale, Viterbo
Layout and cover: Lorenzo Cerrina
English translation: Studio Comunicare, Florence
Photolithography: Fotolito Immagine, Florence
Printing: BO.BA.DO.MA., Florence
ISBN 88-7204-427-8

* The whereabouts of all works mentioned in this book corresponds to their location at the time of publication.

Everything possible has been done to identify the legitimate owners of the copyrights for the individual illustrations. If there have been any involuntary omissions, we will be happy to pay the royalties.

The basilica of San Pietro seen from the valley.

Grand Tour Travelers and the Impoverishment of Tuscania's Artistic Heritage

In the eighteen-forties, George Dennis, a unique combination of eccentric English dilettante, ambassador and scholar, passionately interested in archaeology, visited the cemeteries and cities of Etruria (his fascinating account *The Cities and Cemeteries of Etruria* was published in London in 1848). His words regarding Tuscania were as follows:

"This part of the great plain is diversified by oakwoods,... Tosanella, with its many lofty towers, is the most conspicuous object in the thinly-peopled plain, and may be descried from a great distance. Yet it stands on no eminence, but as usual on the level of the plain, nearly surrounded by profound ravines... its interest lies in its picturesque situation, its Etruscan remains, and its churches, which are choice specimens of the Lombard style. Here and there in the streets is a rich fragment of medieval architecture. The walls of the town are of the same period; no trace of the ancient fortifications remains, except on the adjoining height of San Pietro... The man of antiquarian tastes might spend a week or two of winter pleasantly enough at Toscanella, watching the progress of the excavations, exploring the sepulchres and the picturesque ravines, examining or sketching San Pietro and Sta. Maria... and such quiet pursuits might be diversified by excursions to places in the neighbourhood... to Montefiascone... Bolsena... Viterbo... Vetralla..., Castel d'Asso, Norchia and Bieda..."

This description is just as true now as it ever was, an invitation to discover a city that was once important, with monuments that still hold the remembrance of a glorious past which goes back to antiquity.

The city is situated on a vast tufa upland surrounded by ravines including the ones through which the Marta River and its smaller affluents run, in a complex and haunting landscape that was the setting for important historical events.

When George Dennis went to Tuscania in the 1840s to witness the uncovering of Etruscan tombs and their wealth of tomb furnishings, his main problem was the lack, at the time, of hotels or inns. Dennis had no choice but accept the hospitality of the local butcher who lived near the Campanari family, "whose names are known throughout Europe, wherever a love of Etruscan antiquities has penetrated. ... Some years since, Signor Campanari, wishing to carry on his excavations on a larger scale, set about forming a society or company for the purpose, when the Government (i.e. the Papal government) ...opposed and furthered his design by offering itself as coadjutor.... In the partition of the spoil one party was to make the division, the other selection... and the result was – the Gregorian Museum. ... The Prussian and Bavarian Governments have acted on the same principle; but with the English, says Campanari, it was "the most for our money." This amiable account highlights what was then, as well as later, the principal industry in Roman Tuscia, the trade in Etruscan antiquities – on a grand scale by the large land owners and on a minor scale by the *tombaroli* or tomb robbers, who are still active in the area today. There were countless local finds, often of exceptional importance: an idea can be furnished by the enormous number of sarcophagi that came from the tombs in the necropoli:

50 from the tomb of the Statlana family, 27 from that of the Vipinana family – known as Calcarello, and 33, both whole and fragmentary, from the so-called Grotta della Regina. Of the few still on site, the Curunas family tombs are of particular interest. Most of these objects were scattered to the winds: decorative terracottas from the first half of the 4th century with figures of armed warriors on foot or on chariots are in Munich and Paris, sarcophagi in nenfro (the local stone) with the *Myth of the Niobids* and with a procession of a magistrate and the terracotta urn with the *Dying Adonis*, dating to the 2nd - 1st cent. BC, are in the Museo Etrusco Gregoriano in the Vatican, and the famous ivory dice with the names of the first six Etruscan numbers are in the Cabinet des Médailles in the Bibliothèque National in Paris.

Even if traditionally these famous dice came from Tuscania, we now know that they came from Canino, or even Vulci.

In the Etruscan world dice were sacred in nature. The tale told by Herodotus in the 5th century BC, based on Greek evidence, seems a fairly reliable hypothesis for the arrival of the Etruscans from Anatolia. "In the days of Atys [probably Hatti, that is the Hittite], the son of Manes, [that is the guide, the administrator, from the Hittite verb "manny" and therefore the hero] there was a great famine all over Lydia [in Asia Minor]... It is said that in this plight the Lydians invented dice... which they used to combat hunger as follows. Every two days they played for an entire day, thus distracting attention from the search for food; the next day they did not play and ate. They lived this way for eighteen years. As this disaster did not abate but became

even more severe, the king divided the whole population into two parts, and drew lots with dice between them, one half to remain there and the other to go abroad under the leadership of his son Tyrrhenos. ... After sailing past many countries they arrived in Umbria, where they established towns which they still inhabit. But they changed their name from Lydians to a name taken from that of the king's son who had led them, and after him they called themselves Tyrrhenians".

The arrival of the Lydians/Tyrrhenians was supposedly part of a more general movement in the 12th century BC of peoples (the Peoples of the Sea) who migrated from Anatolia towards the western and southern Mediterranean areas. Mention also appears in Egyptian sources for apparently the Lydians had initially hoped to settle in Egypt. In the 1st century BC, in the Rome of the emperor Augustus, the version presented by Herodotus was rejected by Dionysius of Halicarnassus who claimed that the Etruscans were autochthonous and had not come from the East. It should however be kept in mind that the Dionysian version was particularly in line with the Roman emperor's cultural policies. In Virgil's *Aeneid* it was the Latins, and not the Etruscans, who were supposed to have come from Anatolia (descendents of the Trojans, the enemies of the Greeks). But what Augustus was aiming at above all was to base a sort of 'Italic cultural recovery' on the Etruscans in opposition to the preponderant Greek culture. Etruscan autochthony in Italy was therefore particularly welcome with respect to the theory that had them arrive from the East. Currently there is a tendency to 'merge' the two versions: peoples who arrived from Lydia settled in what was to be Etruria (the Villanovans?) and they merged with the local populations to give rise to a new people and what we know as the Etruscan civilization.

According to Herodotus then, the Lydians brought dice, as well as culture and art, and centuries later, dice were still sacred objects for the Etruscans. Examples are the dice from Tuscania, now in the Cabinet des Médailles in Paris, which had accompanied their owner to the tomb (the birth of a civilization/death as a new journey towards the unknown).

Other important finds from Tuscania now elsewhere are the *roaring lion* and the bronze mirror with *Tagete revealing the secrets of the Disciplina Etrusca to the haruspex Tarchon* (the lore of divination) in the Archaeological Museum in Florence. Dispersion, or in this case more precisely impoverishment, of the original site, was still the rule not all that long ago, and the most important objects from the excavation campaigns in Roman Tuscia were acquired by the Etruscan Museum of Villa Giulia in Rome.

The same fate awaited the medieval and Renaissance majolicas of Tuscania which have been scattered throughout the world. Most of them came from the *"butti"* or domestic refuse pits and pieces by the hundreds came to light particularly during the reconstruction carried out after the earthquake of February 1971. Even before anyone had a chance to identify and study them, they were put on the market and sold through the channels of the abusive antiquarian trade. Information on their provenance has been lost forever and a whole chapter in the History of Italian Majolica has been canceled, even before being written. The production of the Viterbo workshops is still little known and often confused with that of the many Umbrian, Tuscan and Roman centers.

To make things worse, little evidence remains of medieval and Renaissance painting. There are frescoes of various periods in the two major basilicas (San Pietro and Santa Maria Maggiore), in San Silvestro, in San Francesco, in Sant'Agostino, as well as minor fragments that came to light when buildings collapsed in the earthquake. There are no more than a dozen panel paintings of any artistic value, or at least, of documentary interest. Considering the tormented vicissitudes of Tuscania – wars, plunder, and lastly, the systematic spoliation of the convents and patrician palazzi from the last century on – the number of wall paintings and moveable works of art destroyed and dispersed must have been enormous.

The reopening of the Museo Archeologico Nazionale, fascinating despite its small size, is a step in the right direction, at least from the archaeological point of view and the appreciation of the material from Etruscan and Roman tombs still to be found in Tuscania.

Brief History

Little or nothing is known about Tuscania's ancient history, as is true for most Etruscan cities. The first literary mention is to be found in Pliny the Elder, where mention is made of the *Tuscanienses*, the inhabitants of the city. As classical antiquity waned, the town appeared in the *Peutingerian Table* [a topographic map of the various cities of the empire], on the Via Clodia between Blera and Saturnia. Little remains to tell us of the inhabited center and only the necropoli and their rich tomb furnishings bear witness to its importance. In addition to the sarcophagi (in nenfro, the local stone, and in terra-cotta, decorated in low relief and with a reclining figure of the deceased on the cover: the former are the oldest and finest artistically, while the latter are more recent and generally more artisan in nature), objects in bronze, gold, terra-cotta were found. While there are some painted vases, they are curiously scarce, particularly when compared to the countless examples from the nearby Vulci.

One of the best known is the red-figure krater dating to the late 4th century BC, found in Tuscania in the second half of the 19th century, and now in the Museo Civico di Storia e Arte in Trieste. Two demons (the Etruscan *Charu* and *Tuchulcha*) are shown accompanying the deceased to the Netherworld.

In Etruscan times Tuscania was the leading political center of a vast territory scattered throughout with small

View of the center of Tuscania.
Following page: *view of the city walls.*

towns and ancient settlements. The city was in fact one of those Etruscan villages, like the Latin *populi* of pre-Roman Lazio, which represented the continuity of autonomous communities, all the way back to the Bronze Age.

The earliest archaeological evidence dates to the Villanovan Period (9th century BC), before the affirmation of the Etruscan civilization as such, with a settlement located on what would later continue to be the acropolis of the city, the religious site *par excellence* of the center, the hill of San Pietro where the basilica of the same name now stands (outside the inhabited nucleus).

Many objects were found in the ancient acropolis as well as the neighboring necropoli dating to the 8th century BC, when the Etruscans were

present in central Italy (some scholars think in continuity with the Villanovans, others propose a new people who came from outside, from Asia). This then is the period in which a true urban civilization developed in Tuscania.

It is commonly held that the city developed late, although many chamber tombs found in the vicinity belong to the archaic period and in their structure and decoration recall contemporary tombs in Tarquinia, Blera, San Giuliano and San Giovenale. The origins of the Etruscan city can therefore be dated at least to the dawn of the 7th century [but more likely to the 8th]. It probably began as a sanctuary and gradually developed, attaining its zenith between the 4th

and 1st cent. BC, as Tarquinia declined.

The archaic vitality of Tuscania was not followed by a period of decadence, as was so frequently the case in many of the older settlements, but by a long period of continued development. The Etruscan name of the city is not known, but it is likely that the Roman "*Tuscana*" was based on the older name, particularly in consideration of the fact that "Tusc-" is the ancient root of the name the Etruscans (or Tusci) used for themselves. Some have proposed "Tuschna" in an effort to demonstrate the continuity of the name. We know that the Etruscan and then Roman city was much larger than modern-day Tuscania (the acropolis was almost at the center), while the necropoli rose up along the main communication routes, which rayed out in the territory to the neighboring centers. Between the 7th and 6th centuries the center gravitated in the orbit of Tarquinia. Then in the 5th cent. BC Tuscania achieved greater autonomy until it was conquered in the 3rd century BC by the Romans. The city was thus one of the most active centers of inner southern Etruria, thanks above all to its strategic site along one of the fundamental trade routes leading out of Umbria, and from the North to the South as far as Campania. Tuscania also controlled the Marta river valley, with its ancient road for moving the herds from their pastures on the Volsini mountains to the plains towards the sea. Thanks to the exacting of tolls and the control of these communication routes, the urban center was able to amass wealth and expand, especially when the new Via Clodia, built by the Romans (474 BC) on older itineraries, made travel even easier and safer.

The fortunes of the city therefore depended in great part on its ideal geographic location, between the Tyrrhenian shore and the volcanic crater lakes of Bolsena, Vico and Bracciano, on the right bank of the Marta river, emissary of the lake of Bolsena. On a tufa outcrop, like many Etruscan cities, it was bounded by deep ravines, and was the crossing point for the roads from Tarquinia to Bisenzio and from Blera to Statonia. The sea was also no more than

ten miles away, and the city had its own port, called Regas, near Montalto di Castro in a locality now known as Murelle.

One thing the Etruscan cities had in common was that of not being located, for defensive purposes, directly on the coast (where malaria was often present), but always some miles inland, on a height, and with a commercial trading center, often a free port where foreigners, such as the Greeks, might also live, on the shore.

The river to one side and the low hills on which the inhabited center rose and still stands accentuated the unique resemblance of Tuscania with Rome. The Etruscan city was spread out over the hill of San Pietro, rising up sheer over the Marta river. The acropolis was located here, on the highest and most easily defendable point, while the city stretched out over the space still occupied by the town today, inside the perimeter of the walls. A few remains of Etruscan buildings can still be found inside the city, while there are

many necropoli in the surroundings .

Even though Tuscania continued to flourish after the Roman occupation of the region in the 3rd cent. BC, there were no events of note (assigned to the Stellatina tribe, it became a *municipium* in 89 BC after the Social War).

It was at this time that the legend arose that the city was founded by Aeneas's son Ascanius on the site in which a dog with four puppies was whimpering. The myth of its Roman foundation undoubtedly echoed an Etruscan story which connected the founding of Tuscania to the son of the king of a group of Lydian refugees who arrived in central Italy from Anatolia (according to Herodotus). As in Virgil's *Aeneid*, attempts were made in Roman times to claim the Latin rather than Etruscan origin of these foundation myths. The taking of Tuscania by the Romans was anything but easy for the city was allied to Tarquinia. The decisive battle was fought near Orte and seems to have been so bloody that the waters of the Tiber ran red.

Even so, little is left of monuments of this period, almost exclusively limited to remains of *opus reticulatum* [a type of masonry in which individual small square blocks of stone or brick were set into the mortar at a 45° angle to form a net-like pattern] that crop up here and there in the inhabited area. There are also a few ruins of what was once a bath building of Augustan age (1st cent. BC) at the foot of the Colle di San Pietro, known as "il Bagno della Regina" (the Baths of the Queen). Other modest traces have come to light in recent excavations in the Civita quarter, within the inhabited area.

Other remains of some interest include the vestiges of a classical temple on the acropolis under the basilica of San Pietro, while even deeper there are Etruscan tunnels and cisterns which bear witness to the complex stratification of the site. A 3rd century BC sarcophagus, depicting a funeral procession in honor of the magistrate for whom it was made, and now in Rome in the Vatican Museums, comes from the acropolis of Tuscania. The inscriptions on the sarcophagus are all in Etruscan, a language still in use in the early centuries of the Christian era. In accordance with a law of continuity in the siting of places of worship, the church of Santa Maria Maggiore was built on the ruins of a Roman, and perhaps even Etruscan, temple. Masonry structures in *opus reticulatum* have been identified under the floor of the nave. There are Roman remains on the hill known as "del Rivellino" (a rivellino is an outpost of a fortification) where the Town Hall stands as well as down below at its base. Once parts of houses and of a bathing establishment, they tell us that Tuscania had at least two public baths. An urban stretch of the ancient Via Clodia has also been uncovered, and provides significant information on a paved road of Roman times. Of interest too is an inscription of AD 407 which cites a date according to the Christian calendar. Presumably the city, by now converted to Christianity, was still flourishing.

San Pietro on the old hill of the Acropolis.

With the fall of the Roman Empire (AD 476), Tuscania's fate was that of the entire region, overrun by the invading Heruli and Goths, with a weak Byzantine government and the pressure of the advancing Lombards.

Battles and invasions led to a decline in the population and in the 5th century AD the urban center began to recede. Up to about the 10th century the only inhabited area was around the acropolis, the exact opposite of what it is now. In 574, or 569, the city was occupied by the Lombards in whose hands it remained until 774.

The city probably declined until it was almost uninhabited.

It is however not unlikely that given its strategic position of control close to the Byzantine possessions around Rome, Tuscania always remained an important military settlement of the Lombard Duchy of Spoleto. Despite the fact that the Lombards retained control of the city for all of two centuries, there is little evidence of their stay in the city or surroundings, with the exception of a parchment of March 736. Originally from the monastery of San Salvatore on Mount Amiata, it is now in the State Archives in Siena and was drawn up in Tuscania (known as "Toscanella" up to 1911). The text tells us that the brothers Faichisi and Pasquale, whose father was a serf (in Lombard law "aldio") of the Monastery of San Saturnino in Tuscania, agree to do works of "warcisca", another Lombard term which meant work in the fields involving the cutting of the pasturelands. In an earlier document of 595 (twenty years after the Lombard conquest) regarding bishops present at a council, mention is made of "Vibono", the bishop who administered the diocese of Tuscania up to Viterbo. The first church of Santa Maria Maggiore (built on a Roman temple) should therefore date to then, if not shortly before. In the absence of archaeological or material evidence, the few surviving documents hint at a continuity of life in the center in the Lombard period (when it was also the seat of a bishopric). The appearance of terms of Germanic law in the juridical language also demonstrate the influence of Lombard customs in the area. Even in the cities where greater numbers of Lombards settled, they used the precedent structures (dwellings, walls, religious centers). The Lombards had no architects of their own and in the 8th century Paul the Deacon, their most famous historian, informs us that in the cities of Northern Italy they lived in small houses, but above all in areas set against the walls, in wood and stone huts, which they called "*case*" (and not using the Roman word *domus*) and that, in general, they settled in the area to devote themselves to animal husbandry. Lombard Tuscania seems to have been no exception to the rule. The first cathedral of Santa Maria Maggiore with its three apses (although only the central apse projects externally) seems to date to this period. Architectural models of this kind, of Byzantine derivation, appear in Italy in the 8th century at the end of the Lombard reign and the beginning of Frankish influence.

Tuscania was then involved in the more general events which eventually, in the course of eight centuries, led to the constitution of the Patrimony of St. Peter, that is the State of the Church (which began when the Lombard king Liutprand donated the city of Sutri to Pope Gregory II in 728).

When Charlemagne's donation enlarged the State of the Church, Toscanella/Tuscania also became a papal dominion (778). The absence of historical sources relating to the Lombard period have led some to conclude that the city practically disappeared. But the minute Tuscania passed under papal rule, information was once more forthcoming. This was the beginning of a period of prosperity for the town, politically connected to the territories of Lazio in a single state. A profound change took place in the ecclesiastical and topographical hierarchy of the city. The basilica of Santa Maria Maggiore, old bishop's seat, lost its standing as cathedral, although it remained an important city church and was rebuilt and enlarged (in 852). The important basilica of San Pietro, now elevated to bishop's seat, was built on the ruins of the old pagan temple on the acropolis, although Santa Maria Maggiore continued to be the baptismal church for centuries.

The town plan of Tuscania thus changed in function of a new political/religious polarity: with respect to Santa Maria Maggiore, located in a flatter area near the territorial routes, the new papal government preferred to strengthen the bishop's citadel which once more was centered on the ancient height of the acropolis which, in addition to being a religious center, was also fortified. The relationship between city and power was thus radically changed. The political center was no longer located within the urban fabric but was an isolated fortified area which would stress the role of Bishop-Prince. Rome apparently wanted to make sure that the bishop was not too closely tied to the old Lombard government.

The political situation remained uncertain for a long time in the struggles between the Papacy and the Empire, for Tuscania was located, as in Lombard times, right on the border between the two possessions. The residence of the apostolic vicar or the imperial governor in the city always had to be easy to defend, as well as reflect the power and economic and artistic wealth of whatever side was at the moment in power, either papal or imperial.

This is why, for example, in the middle of the 11th century the cathedral of San Pietro was completely rebuilt in line with the most advanced aesthetic norms of the time, a demonstration of the wealth of Tuscania and its pre-eminence in upper Lazio with regards to the neighboring imperial possessions.

The period was marked by internecine struggles for power between the feudal aristocracy in the countryside - which did not recognize papal sovereignty until the time of Pope Innocent II (1198-1216) - and the Church, the Empire and then the Commune. Their opponents, or external allies, were, in typical medieval fashion, the Lombard kingdom, the Carolingian dynasty or the Holy Roman Empire. Town planning and art, as well as the economy of Tuscania, reflected these various vicissitudes. A free Commune, subject to or rebelling against the Church and dominated in the baronial period by the Anguillara and the Aldobrandeschi, it was located on the frontiers between the Church and the Empire, between the old Byzantine and papal dominions and those of the Lombards, and kept passing from one side to the other.

In order to ensure its political control over these areas, in 1193 papal authority elevated neighboring Viterbo, a safer town, to a bishopric, sharply reducing the ecclesiastical jurisdiction of Tuscania. This competition between the two cities was played out on all levels until Viterbo, favored by the vicinity of the Via Cassia, developed more rapidly than Tuscania and became the neuralgic center of papal power in the area. The animosity between the two cities frequently flared up. In 1213, citizens of Tuscania beat up two Viterbesi. Revenge was not long in coming. That night a gang of Viterbesi attacked Tuscania and a riot broke out. Over two hundred Tuscanesi, surprised in their sleep, were captured and carried in procession to Viterbo bound to the horns of billy goats.

By the end of the 13th century Viterbo had won out. But this rivalry, that was economical and political as well, continued on into the 18th and 19th century in the field of culture. Attempts were made to demonstrate that one city was older than the other and at a certain point the Viterbesi even took over 'the Roman name and the history of the neighboring Tuscania" which, objectively, was older. In 1887 Cesare Pinzi put an end to these contentions, pointing out that each of

View of the basilica of San Pietro from the apse end.

the two sister cities had its glories. Pinzi also settled the question of which bishopric was older. Since many cities in the area – including Tuscania – were at the time semi-destroyed, the foundation bull of the Viterbo bishopric (1193), sent by Pope Celestine III, "has not come down to us". Other documents, however, including the papal bull of Innocent III of 1207, have survived. These demonstrate that the original bishopric was in Tuscania and was not moved to Viterbo until the end of the 12th century.

The position of Tuscania within the papal possessions could never be counted on. Pope Innocent III reconquered it at the beginning of the 13th century. After still another expedition, Pope Boniface VIII (1294-1303) took the rebellious city back. The tradition, handed down by the Tuscanese historian Campanari, that the Pope wanted to humiliate Tuscania after having brought it back into the fold by giving it the more 'commonplace' and 'meaner' name of "Toscanella" dates from these times. Actually the name was already in use in the early Middle Ages, but most likely the Latin name Tuscania, continued to be used in official documents. The papal document to truncate any desire the Tuscanesi might have to reconnect to the ancient secular *imperium* of Rome and therefore rebel against the Church, made the vernacular name official. The identification of the name of the city also played a part in the political controversies. In memory of its reconquest by Pope Boniface VIII, a plaque was set into the wall inside the Capitoline Palace in Rome, with the inscription *"tu Toscanella fuisti/ of dirum dampnata nefas"* (Pinzi).

It was not until 1911, forty years after the Unification of Italy, that the city, which for centuries had been part of the Papal State, took back its old name of "Tuscania", to which a bronze plaque on the outer staircase of the present Town Hall bears witness.

In 1102 Tuscania was included in the imperial legacy of the Countess Matilda of Canossa. Frederick Barbarossa then appropriated the city in the course of a war with the neighboring Viterbo. In 1207 Pope Innocent III confirmed its municipal freedom. When Tuscania then became a free Commune in the 13th century, thanks to the weakness of both papal and imperial power, the city flourished economically and demographically, despite the internecine struggles between opposing factions for control of the city government. The center expanded from the hill of San Pietro to that of Santa Maria Maggiore and it once more became a city characterized by various centers set on several hills that were connected by inhabited areas. This was when the fortified Town Hall was built on the Rivellino (where the Town Hall is today) and the great city wall with five gates was raised. Once again, as the political situation changed so did the physical layout of Tuscania. The popes had built a fortified center, focussed on the cathedral of San Pietro and the residence of

the bishop-prince. The imperial governors also found this setup to their advantage.

With the free Commune however, the hill where the new Town Hall stood, surrounded by walls of its own, as well as the entire city center, gained in importance with respect to the fortified acropolis. Patrician palaces outdid each other in height, protected by the wide walls, and these tower houses lent Tuscania the typical aspect of a medieval city. As elsewhere, the city was constantly involved in fighting between the Guelph (pro-papal) and the Ghibelline (imperial and subsequently for communal freedom) factions and the families fortified their houses.

As papal power disintegrated and the multiple partisan forces came to the fore during the years of papal exile in Avignon (1305-1377) Tuscania found itself prey for the factions and the object of ferocious struggles. In 1353 it fell under the rule of Giovanni di Vico, whose powerful family held the urban prefecture in Rome as a hereditary right, and which was aiming at extending its possessions in the territories in Tuscia over which the Patrimony of St. Peter had ruled for centuries. The following year it was reconquered by Cardinal Gil de Albornoz, sent to Italy as Legate by Pope Innocent VI (1357-1362), with the intent of restoring papal authority.

With the Schism of the West (1378-1415) and the nomination of two rival popes (the Pope and the Antipope), the times continued to be troubled and Tuscania was frequently raided by mercenary troops. In 1407 the town was sacked by Paolo Orsini, captain in the service of Pope Gregory XII, when his troops had not received their due pay from the pope. In

1414 it was taken by Angelo Brogio da Lello known as il Tartaglia, who kept it for seven years till 1421.

Actually Tartaglia, at the time in the hire of the papal legate, had taken Tuscania from Paolo Orsini as early as 1408. In 1413 however Tartaglia, who was also a soldier of fortune, abandoned the papal camp and went over into the service of King Ladislav. The following year he changed sides again and officially obtained the possession of Tuscania which he already controlled anyway.

In addition to building new fortified structures and his own palace (all that is left today, in addition to the coat of arms, are a few two-light windows incorporated into later buildings and the tower gate of Lavello; in the 19th century there was also a coat of arms inside the church of Santa Maria della Rosa), Tartaglia promoted a humanistic court centered on the figure of the Sienese poet Simone Serdini known as Saviozzo (who later died a suicide in prison, after having disagreed with his Lord).

Tartaglia was beheaded in 1421 by his rival Attendolo Sforza who thus conquered the city. The people tore down Tartaglia's palace as reprisal for the deplorable way he had treated them.

Sacked anew in 1435 by Francesco Sforza, the following year it was taken by Cardinal Vitelleschi who, as punishment for this umpteenth revolt against the Holy See, had most of the fortifications torn down, as well as the walls and the neighboring castles that had participated in the rebellion.

When Vitelleschi also fell into disgrace, in 1443 Tuscania defnitively passed under papal rule, the principal

The Hill of San Pietro (Ainsley, 1842).

center of which in the area was Viterbo. In 1494 Annio da Viterbo had the collection of Etruscan sarcophagi installed in the Palazzo dei Priori in Viterbo. This was the beginning of a civic Etruscan Museum and it is probable that material from Tuscania was also included.

In the Tolfa Mountains (near Tarquinia, a few dozen kilometers from Tuscania), important mines of alum had in the meanwhile been discovered. This mineral was used as a catalyzing agent in tanning hides, in fixing textile colors, in stabilizing gold and silver as well as in producing heat refractory materials. The mines had already been known in Etruscan times, but in the Middle Ages, in part because of the continuous struggles, they had never been adequately exploited. Their re-discovery meant little as such for

the area economically, for the mines were managed directly by the Apostolic Chamber, which pocketed all the profits. The side effects were however considerable for trade increased and attracted merchants who set up whole colonies of outsiders and also became patrons of the arts. Various states also set their eyes on this highly profitable activity.

But the worst calamity, after half a century of peace, hit Tuscania at the turn of the 15th century.

The city had brilliantly withstood the siege of the Duke of Calabria, on behalf of the King of Naples, in 1486, despite the fact that his army was furnished with terrible "war machines". The most important of these were the *vinee*, or cats, already in use among

the ancient Romans. This "machine" was a sort of moveable shelter covered with grates which allowed the attacking troops to approach the walls with their battering rams without being hit by the defenders. Despite the fact that the Neapolitan soldiers had been enticed by the promise of plundering a "very rich" city, the hilly layout of Tuscania made it impossible for them to use their *vinee* to the best advantage. In addition, the Tuscanesi threw down stones and beams from on high which made holes in the grates. The walls were solid and impregnable and without artillery a siege had little hope of success. After hours of battle, the Neapolitan encampment was removed and the city freed.

In 1493 Pope Alexander VI made his triumphal entrance into the city. In the same year the city greeted the election of Alexander Farnese to cardinal with great rejoicing. Farnese was born in Canino, a hamlet subject to the Commune of Tuscania (in the traditional "Ager Tuscaniensis") with the annual payment of a sum established by precise pacts. Upon his election, the City sent its fellow citizen in Rome a gift of two silver cups, as well as congratulations (Campanari). This marked the beginning of direct contacts between Tuscania and the Farnese family and was to lead to important changes in the urban layout of the city.

A plague in 1494 decimated the population. The following year it was laid waste by the troops of the French king Charles VIII, who massacred the population and semi-destroyed the inhabited area.

Actually the sack, which remained famous in Lazio for a long time on account of its brutality, was carried out without the authorization of the king who was residing in Viterbo at the time. Charles VIII had agreed to have part of his army sojourn in Sutri, while some of the legions, commanded by the so-called Gran Bastardo, were to continue on to Tuscany. When these troops arrived outside the walls of Tuscania looking for lodgings and provisions, they asked the Rectors for permission to enter the city. Refusal unleashed the fury of the French troops who were armed with powerful cannons and not the *vinee* and battering rams of the Duke of Calabria. They broke down the walls, burned the gates and laid the city waste. They sacked the houses and killed all the men they found. Only those who had taken refuge in the towers survived. The French troops remained for five days and when the priors of Viterbo heard of the catastrophe, they went in embassy to Charles VII (who was still in their city) and requested him to free

Tuscania and the prisoners. The City of Viterbo also sent aid to the Tuscanesi in the form of food, doctors and medicines. There were about eight hundred dead.

It took the city a long time to recover from the catastrophe. But it was also one that conditioned the subsequent urban development.

At this point Tuscania had lost its strategic importance. The State of the Church was stabilizing its possessions towards Umbria, so that Tuscania no longer held a role as an important border center between various warring Seignorias and territories. Once the coastal zone had also been pacified, the old Via Aurelia and the Cassia constituted the main transportation routes, while Viterbo was the city that the popes had definitively designated as their neuralgic and directional center in Upper Lazio.

The acropolis/hill of San Pietro, the area most heavily devastated by the French artillery, was abandoned, as was the hill of Rivellino (where the Town Hall was) and the Sette Cannelle. The city was rebuilt on a more circumscribed area and the cathedral was transferred to the church of Santa Maria della Rosa.

Once more, and this time radically, the site of the principal religious pole of Tuscania changed. The bishop's seat had previously 'migrated' from the plateau of the church of Santa Maria Maggiore to the acropolis of San Pietro, both in the southern part of the inhabited area. It was now shifted to the opposite or north side of the city, to Santa Maria della Rosa, where a fresco of the *Madonna of Salvation* celebrated the withdrawal of the troops of Charles VIII. This was the

largest religious building within the reconstructed medieval nucleus, although the old Palazzo del Podestà (more or less in the area where the Town Hall in Piazza Basile now stands) remained outside.

Parts of the city were therefore rebuilt in line with the preexisting fabric of the northern zone, and then, in the 1500s, in line with a new grid plan along which dignified sixteenth century buildings went up.

The guidelines for the rebirth of the center were dictated by a purely local situation and the two distinct units which emerged can still be clearly identified. The intricate pattern of streets in the NE part of the city harks back to the original medieval settlement rebuilt in the early sixteenth century. The expansion of the NW zone, subsequent but still sixteenth century, is characterized by a network of orthogonal streets which betray the influence of modern Renaissance theories of town planning.

This latter area of the Poggio was where the local nobility lived (the Pocci, the Consalvi) and it still looks as it did then, centered around the present Cathedral (Duomo) of San Giacomo.

The moving, in 1572, of the Cathedral from Santa Rosa to San Giacomo, in the modern part, once more reflected the changing urban hierarchy of the various zones. As soon as the devastation the French troops left in their wake had been repaired, the Cathedral was moved to the old medieval area of the Poggio. With the sixteenth century expansion of the city, the new quarter (also inhabited in earlier times) became more important. It seemed only logical that the most important religious center of Tuscania be transferred there as desired by Cardinal Gambara, bishop and entrusted with the management of the papal policies *in situ*. What the Farnese did, through Giovan Francesco Gambara, was fundamental in promoting this transformation. Ever since 1537 the Farnese had directly controlled the neighboring Duchy of Castro, but they had already affirmed themselves in the upper Viterbo area as early as the late 15th century. This territory had been curtailed from the *Ager Tuscaniensis*, the municipal territory of Tuscania, from which the cities of the Duchy depended back in Antiquity. The Farnese, from Canino, had always been citizens of Tuscania. Although not actually a part of the Farnese possessions, Tuscania was however indirectly included (the border passed a few kilometers from the center), thanks also to the influence of the noble family. The entire territory of Upper Lazio was administered, as Legate, by Cardinal Alessandro, nephew of Alessandro, the future Pope Paul II. The bishopric of the Viterbo-Tuscania diocese was moreover also assigned to Cardinal Gambara, affiliated with the Farnese.

The concepts of urban expansion which Gambara applied to Tuscania, on behalf of Alessandro Farnese, exemplified what was done in other Farnese cities. The original nucleus was enlarged, although it remained within the old walls, by tracing one or more main streets with minor streets going off at right angles to form a grid centered on a new (or renewed) religious pole, while the building lots were settled by the working classes or those closely tied to the Farnese family. This is what happened in Tuscania, but a similar operation was carried out in grand style in Parma (with several avenues in the zone across the river); in Piacenza, also by Cardinal Gambara (1543), where the boulevard was immediately known as "Stradone Gambara". And in Viterbo too, the other 'bishop's' city in Upper Lazio: the Farnesine road (Strada Nuova now Via Cavour) was opened in 1573 by Cardinal Farnese himself, papal legate, who adopted ideas previously used by his uncle, Paul II, (Via dei Baullari in Rome) and by Galeazzo Alessi in the Via Nuova in Perugia. In 1570 the Legate, through the cardinal/bishop Gambara, also had the new facade of the Viterbo Cathedral of San Lorenzo rebuilt, very like that of the Cathedral of Tuscania (thus stressing the ties between the two religious centers of San Giacomo and San Lorenzo). Ten years earlier, in 1560, the nave of the Cathedral of Viterbo finally received its new tribune, designed by the Farnese architect Antonio da Sangallo. Although the fountain in the Piazza della Rocca (1566) and the Porta Faulle (1568) in Viterbo were unquestionably designed by Jacopo Barozzi known as Vignola, questions remain as to whether he also was responsible for the Stradone and the facade of the cathedral. Documents however do exist certifying the presence of the architect in the vicinity of the Lake of Bolsena, for works in the Duchy of Castro, several times between 1562 and 1573.

Vignola renovated the villa of Caprarola (also near Viterbo) for Cardinal Alessandro Farnese and was then also employed by Gambara, who was related to the Farnese and owed them his success, for his Villa of Bagnaia (later Villa Lante) near Viterbo.

As a result of the presence of the Farnese and Gambara's episcopate (from 1566 to 1576), Tuscania was intimately involved in their urban and territorial policies. There is a great deal of historical evidence of a direct tie between the City of Tuscania and its powerful fellow citizens. In 1541 the City deliberated to elect Cardinal Alessandro Farnese, nephew of the pope, as its protector (Campanari). The decision of the Cardinal to repair the walls, still mostly half destroyed, and to have the streets, which were in beaten earth, paved, dates to 1553. Officially this was on behalf of the Pope, but the pope was at the time Marcellus II Cervini, former Farnese secretary. The Farnese also administered other property, in addition to their own palace in the city (of which unfortunately we have no history), as the settlement of a controversy between a citizen of Tuscania and the Farnese duchess of Parma tells us. In 1565 the City requested the intercession and aid of Cardinal Farnese, as well as the Tuscan Girolamo Maccabei, bishop of the Farnese Duchy of Castro, to obtain the pope's pardon after the murder of the Gonfaloniere del Popolo (a pardon which invariably arrived in 1568: Campanari).

Thanks to the modifications of the town plan sponsored by the Farnese and Gambara, Tuscania received still another new look, although it was not as sensational an event as in the past.

In the sixteenth century the Church was unifying its territories by assimilating the last of the baronial powers. By the middle of the 17th century unification was achieved when the Farnese Duchy of Castro and Ronciglione was suppressed and its capital, Castro, destroyed. Tuscania was demoted to the rank of a tranquil provincial city of the Papal State, and nothing of great importance happened except for the building of a few monuments, such as new 17th-18th century fountains and small palazzi. Subsequent centuries have added little to the aspect of the city. In the 19th century Piazza Francesco Basile, where the Palazzo Campanari and the Town Hall

The ruins of the Rivellino castle.

tand, was restructured. The growth in population and the building development of the 1900s that has gradually moved out radially outside the walls, have not greatly altered the ancient core of the city. This stable equilibrium partially upset in 1954 by the collapse of the tower of the Rivellino, which swept away several buildings below, including the 19th century Municipal Theatre), was hard hit on the dramatic evening of February 6, 1971. A swift but catastrophic earthquake overwhelmed the city, with enormous consequences for the historic center where entire quarters collapsed either totally or partially and almost all the monuments, including the basilicas of San Pietro and Santa Maria Maggiore, suffered damage of varying degree. Fortunately, a series of favorable circumstances in these adversities of chance, limited the number of victims.

Tuscania once more made the news in the early 1960s with Pier Paolo Pasolini's film, *Uccellacci e Uccellini* (*The Hawks and the Sparrows*), interpreted by the famous Italian comedian, Totò.

On February 6, 1971, chaos erupted into the peaceful life of Tuscania. The disaster that followed two earthquakes was of apocalyptic proportions in this delicate historical context. Over 500 buildings were damaged, 70% of those in the city. The enormity of the drama was immediately clear for by this time Italian culture had matured the conviction that the term monument included not only the finest buildings, but the fabric of the old dwellings as well, the streets, the squares. And that the survival of a center depended mainly on how many people lived there. National and local institutions were instantly mobilized, defining the concepts and principles to be used in the work of reconstruction. Riccardo Pacini highlighted the fact that "the problem is composed of that

unrivalled complex of the old center, composed of medieval and Renaissance houses, with simple plastered facades enriched with portals, windows, elegant loggias and stone cornices.... It is impossible to set up a scale of importance, for the less important buildings are the necessary frame for the more important ones. Certainly the appearance...which had come down to us thanks to these unique testimonials of a harmonious building development will in part be lost.... In many cases the only thing left of a dwelling is the facade, while the inside has collapsed. In others there is the pulverization of the mortars on the walls themselves". This concept is also repeated by Guglielmo Matthiae: "The ambience of a historical center owes its charm to a sum of minor elements which if torn out of context have a minimum and perhaps even negligible value, but which concur efficaciously and certainly above their intrinsic value when seen as a whole.... To allow demolition and reconstruction would mean compromising Tuscania… it is better to leave old facades standing, with the opportune consolidation, not to allow the colors or architectural lines to be modified, leaving the volumes within the pre-earthquake limits… repairing the empty houses, inside, in line with modern needs…. It will therefore not be by building modern apartment buildings outside of the historical center that one can help those hit by the quake, favoring the abandonment… even if it is certainly more difficult technically and more costly to save the ancient center". A list of the damage suffered by the more important buildings also sounded like a report from the front. The covering and part of the apse of the church of San Pietro had collapsed, taking with it the 13th century fresco of Roman school depicting the *Ascension of Christ*. Guglielmo Matthiae noted with particular regret that the loss of this stylistically fine fresco, an important page in 12th century history, was beyond repair, adding that the fragments were being collected and that attempts were being made to identify them. Pasquale Rotondi was more specific in his description "In San Pietro the conch of the apse with the *Ascension* has fallen while the rest of the scene, with the *Apostles*, is damaged and tot-

Via degli Archi.

tering as a result of the rotation of the wall, so that the triumphal arch is in danger of becoming detached. The only way these frescoes can be saved, given the precariousness of the static aspect, is by detaching the plaster from the wall…. But since the medieval plaster in Tuscania is very thin and poor in lime, these frescoes are extremely fragile and when they fall they break up into minute fragments which makes recomposition very difficult". The Basilica itself was unstable in many points, and much had fallen

together with the cornices, as well as the rose window of the facade. The pieces were immediately collected covered and protected until they could be put together again by the experts from the Istituto Centrale del Restauro in Rome. The vault of the crypt was also severely damaged. The bishop's lodgings near the basilica housed the Etruscan Museum and these finds, in view of the damage suffered by the building, were immediately moved (the museum is now in the former convent of the Madonna del Riposo).

The situation of Santa Maria Maggiore was also dramatic, with severe damage to the roof and above all the apse. The nave had been opened in several places and detached from the back wall, many mural paintings had fallen. It was therefore a difficult stabilization of the walls. Riccardo Pacini supplied a rundown of the drama in the principal buildings of the historical center: "in Santa Maria della Rosa the facade has become separated from the building… the chapel with the polyptych by Giulio Pierino d'Amelia is severely damaged. In San Leonardo the roof has fallen in; in San Silvestro the bell tower has suffered severe damage. The Cathedral of San Giacomo is in a disastrous state: the cupola above the altar is gravely damaged, the three chapels have collapsed or are about to collapse. The 14th century overhanging steps (*profferlo*) have however come through as have the paintings by Sparapane da Norcia. Most of the towers of Tartaglia of Lavello and the Rivellino have come through well". And Pasquale Rotondi figured that about seven hundred square meters of frescoes had been damaged.... The Sparapane chapel in San Francesco has cracks and color has detached. The *Tree of Jesse* in San Silvestro is almost intact, while the church of the Monastery of San Paolo is in such a state that the interior is not even accessible. Of a surface of seven hundred square meters of damaged frescoes, about three hundred will have to be detached, while the rest will have to be consolidated where they are. The *Road to Calvary* of the 15th century in the Ospedale di Santa Croce, is damaged. All the paintings and monumental furnishings were immediately removed and taken to Viterbo, even if the damage suffered by the movable panels and furnishings is easy to repair". It has taken years for them to return to Tuscania and some still have not yet come home.

Those in charge had no doubts as to what was to be done: the historical center was not to be abandoned, with the reconstruction of a 'new' Tuscania, nor should the population suffer difficulties in the reconstruction work. Riccardo Pacini pointed out that "the earthquake had struck in a way that was hard to remedy...The buildings restored would no longer, in part, be the authentic buildings, as they had come down to us; the current intervention would be added to that of past centuries, however their basic nature would be recomposed, without falsification and in line with the most up-to-date methods of the restoration of monuments... In restoration all care will be taken to intervene without falsification and without discord". Guglielmo Matthiae stated that "it was necessary to work on the historical center in such a way that the reconstruction works did no more damage than that already inflicted by the earthquake. Sift through the rubble and recover before the material is sent to the dump so that all the smallest elements can be put back in their original place ... and thus every trace of this disaster can be cancelled".

The fate of the city which had seemed without repair, not so much because of the material damage but because this natural catastrophe had profoundly altered the socioeconomic and urban structure, now took a turn for the better. With a timeliness rare in Italy on the occasion of calamities of this sort, opportune measures and precise laws allowed the reconstruction of the city in its original aspect and the restoration of the monuments. So much so that ten years after the quake (1981) Tuscania had almost completely regained its traditional look. Despite the ruinous events of the past, the city is still distinguished as a center of unique artistic interest thanks to the well-preserved town layout, a few outstanding medieval monuments and a connecting fabric of minor buildings which give it its particular character.

Now, thirty years after the earthquake, the balance sheet of reconstruction can be considered almost definitive (even if various works still are absent). To be noted is that, on the basis of historiographical studies which have always favored the medieval history of Tuscania, restoration and reconstruction too tended to favor the neo-medieval aspect of the center and its monuments, preferring the finds from that period and destroying with a certain nonchalance evidence of later periods (especially in discovering new painterly evidence), reconstructing what they thought they presumably originally looked like in that Medieval period, although without stylistic imitation.

THE WALLS

The city walls, as well as the look-out towers and the city gates, continue to bear witness to Tuscania's past of wars and warring factions. The walls around the hill of San Pietro were never rebuilt after the damage inflicted on them by Cardinal Vitelleschi and the troops of Charles VIII, although it was the look-out towers which particularly struck Dennis. Of particular interest are the *Porta San Marco* which still has its defensive structures and is comparable to the San Biele tower in Viterbo and the *Porta del Poggio*, which is much later, surmounted by the clock tower. There are also a few *towers* of the medieval fortified palazzi inside the city such as the *Palazzo del Rivellino*.

In Etruscan times the city was completely surrounded by defensive walls of which noticeable traces remain near the basilicas of San Pietro and of Santa Maria Maggiore. The regularity of the tufa blocks employed testifies to their rather late date, whereas the first set of city walls of this Tyrrhenian city were in what is known as polygonal masonry, consisting of large rough-hewn irregular blocks. The walls were repeatedly destroyed and torn down up to the 15th century when Cardinal Vitelleschi (on the order of the pope) decreed a more systematic demolition in line with Pope Eugene's policy of destroying all the fortifications in the area, considered symbols of the dangerous Ghibelline aspirations (this party, present in all cities in the early Middle Ages, opposed the papal power in favor of annexation to the Empire or communal freedom) and possible infiltration of the rebels in the church. The Cardinal thus had the walls of Tuscania as well as the

Porta San Marco seen from the outside.

Fortress of Viterbo torn down. (Curiously enough, the fortress was rebuilt in 1457 to become the seat of the Popes or their legates.). Eugene IV countered this policy of destruction by a program for the restoration of the principal religious buildings used as bishop's headquarters, as poles of ecclesiastical power. An example is the basilica of San Pietro in Tuscania.

The inner facade of Porta San Marco.

Porta del Poggio with its clock.

From the necropoli to the Etruscan finds

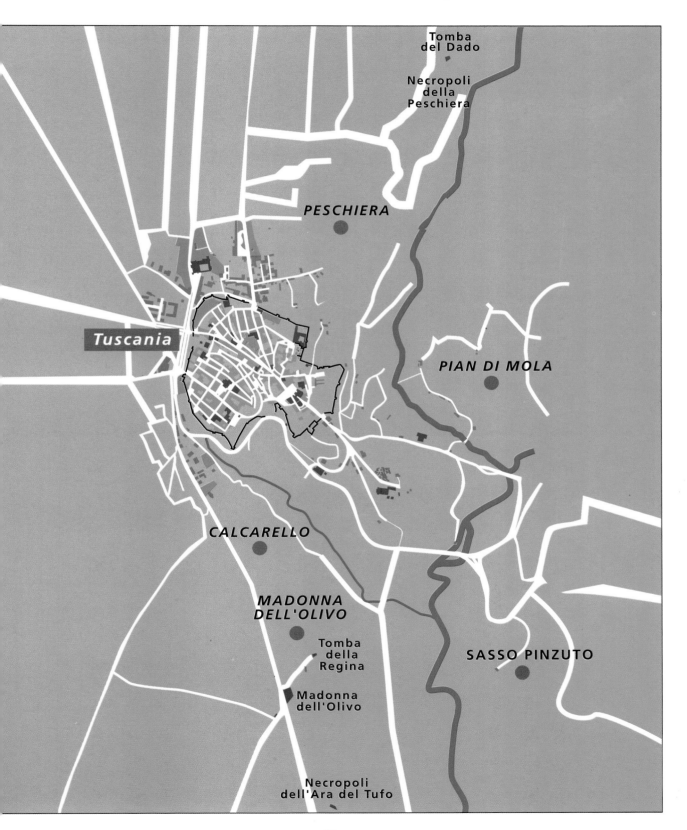

Tomba
del Dado

Necropoli
della
Peschiera

PESCHIERA

Tuscania

PIAN DI MOLA

CALCARELLO

*MADONNA
DELL'OLIVO*

Tomba
della
Regina

Madonna
dell'Olivo

SASSO PINZUTO

Necropoli
dell'Ara del Tufo

While remains of Etruscan buildings within the city are scarce, there are many necropoli in the vicinity, although they lack tombs as interesting as those in Tarquinia, Norchia or Castel d'Asso.

The tour can begin with these necropoli and end with the Museo Archeologico Nazionale, created in Tuscania as a result of the finds of the late 1960s and the 1970s.

The necropoli surrounding the city are vast, although not all are open to the public. They were used in various periods and can also be divided up according to date. Some of them include tombs which became famous for their architectural elements, others for the wealth of the tomb furnishings. The most important cemeteries are those with rock-cut tombs, dug out of the tufa banks to form a jutting facade. There are house-shaped tombs or cube shaped "die" tombs, half-cubes with a portico, some are cut halfway into the rock, others shaft or *pozzetto* tombs meant to contain only the cinerary urn, and bare hypogeums with ogival parts, collective pits, colombaria of Roman times and irregular structures. This gives us an idea of the variety of tomb types used by the Etruscans and by the Romans up to the late settlements of Antiquity.

The necropoli of **Le Scalette**, **San Lazzaro** and **San Giusto** have chamber tombs, pit tombs, shaft tombs with cinerary urns dating to the 8th and 7th centuries BC (in **San Giusto** there are some tombs, dating to the 7th and 6th centuries BC, where slabs were used for the covering. These may however have been reused later for the burial of the lower classes). The necropolis of **Sasso Pinzuto** (datable to between the 7th and 6th centuries BC by the tomb furnishings) contained rich finds, with an abundance of vases in *bucchero*, the typical dark colored Etruscan pottery which imitated metal ware. In **Castelluzza**, in the direction of Marta, the tombs display various kinds of decoration with small beams, as well as carved false doors and windows (5th-4th cent. BC). The necropoli of **Pian di Mola** (chamber tombs with a wealth of terracotta sarcophagi) and **Calcarello** (pit tombs dating from the 7th cent. BC to the 2nd-1st cent. BC) belong to the Etruscan-Roman period. Other necropoli are to be found in localities **Doganello**, **Sughereto** and **San Giuliano**, testifying to the population density of Tuscania and its territory.

The most important of the cemeteries is without question that of the **Madonna dell'Olivo**, spread out over a vast area overlooking the river Marta and still being investigated.

Reconstruction of a tomb from Tuscania in the London exhibition of 1837.

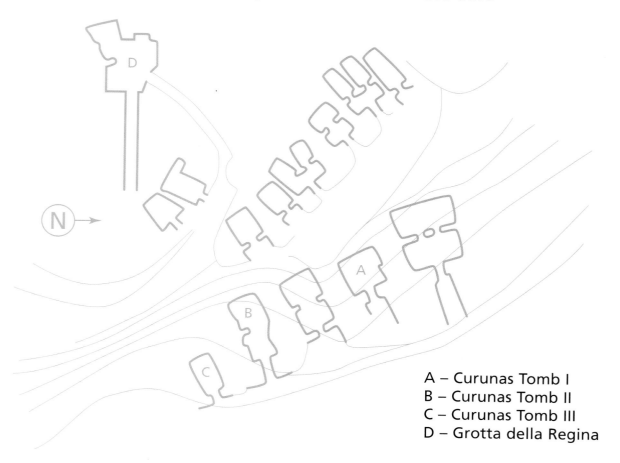

A – Curunas Tomb I
B – Curunas Tomb II
C – Curunas Tomb III
D – Grotta della Regina

Church of the Madonna dell'Olivo

This suburban church is an elegant example of Renaissance architecture.

The church of Santa Maria dell'Olivo was turned into a monumental structure between the late 15th and early 16th centuries, probably after the passage of the troops of Charles VIII in 1495. Since the devotional site stood outside the walls it probably escaped being shelled by the French. It is likely that the humanistic restructuration was based on an older pre-existant shrine. Little is known about this transformation, except for miracles attributed to an image of the Madonna in an older chapel dedicated to the Blessed Columbanus. This ties it

in with the founding of the suburban sanctuary of the Madonna della Quercia in Viterbo, for which, from 1470 on, the town of Tuscania had also contributed economically (in the duplication of the bishop's seat, the relationship of Viterbo to Tuscania was like the sanctuary of the Madonna della Quercia to Santa Maria dell'Olivo). The church may also have been enlarged thanks to the initiative of the cardinal of Tuscania, Alessandro Farnese, and in Tuscan forms since Farnese was closely connected to the Florentine culture. After all, with a special deliberation, when he was elected cardinal (1493), the Town had sent him two silver cups, as well as their congratulations (Campanari), confirming

their ties with their illustrious fellow-citizen.

If Santa Maria dell'Olivo did have Farnese as patron, then mention must also be made of the involvement of the cardinal, as Legate of the Marches, in the Palazzo dei Legati and the Loggia dei Mercanti in Macerata (1504) and the work of the Florentine architect Giuliano da Maiano, whose 'partner' Neri di Bicci had already carried out at least one commission for the Farnese. Nor should it be forgotten that around the 1490s the famous Florentine architect Giuliano da San Gallo was commissioned by Cardinal Giovanni dei Medici – son of Lorenzo the Magnificent and the future Pope Leo X – to renovate the cathedral of Bolsena,

Santa Cristina. He also had close ties with the Farnese. In Sangallo's notebook (*Taccuino*) there are drawings of the well known Viterbo Terme del Bullicame, not far from Tuscania (at Bagno delle Bussette). He apparently also advised on the building of the cathedral of San Lorenzo in Viterbo (which, considering the duplication of the seats of the single Bishopric, was of considerable importance for Tuscania). Another fact to be kept in mind is that Pope Julius II, who passed through Tuscania in 1505, contributed funds for the city churches (and once more bestowed attention on the cathedral of Viterbo).

The plan of the building and its parts in any case are strongly reminiscent of architecture by Francesco di Giorgio Martini.

Necropolis of the Madonna dell'Olivo

Spread out on three levels set against a slope, the necropolis was already known

Top to bottom: *back and facade of the church of the Madonna dell'Olivo.*

Interior.

to the Campanari family. It was the object of new study in 1967 when the Tomb of the Amazons (with the relative sarcophagus) and Curunas Tomb I were discovered. In 1970 Curunas Tombs II and III were identified, bringing the number of sarcophagi found to twelve. These particularly fine examples (now in the Museo Nazionale in Tuscania) were decorated with portraits of the deceased. There are at least thirteen other tombs on these levels (also found in 1970), with two three-chamber tombs, dating to the 4th – 2nd century BC, in which bronze objects as well as about thirty sarcophagi were found. Some of these objects are in the Museum in Tuscania and some are in Villa Giulia in Rome.

The so-called *Tomb* or *Grotta della Regina* is located under the church of the Madonna dell'Olivo.

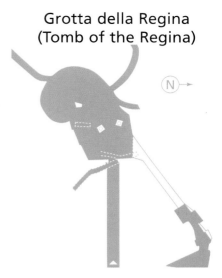

Grotta della Regina
(Tomb of the Regina)

Grotta della Regina
(Grotto of the Queen)

This vast labyrinthine tomb has pillars cut into the rock, and is located a few kilometers from the town, beneath the church of the Madonna dell'Olivo. The name comes from the figure of a woman

Top to bottom: *an untouched tomb discovered in the area of Tuscania and the necropolis of the Madonna dell'Olivo.*

originally painted on the walls and no longer visible.

Contemporary archaeologists were however highly dubious with regards to the painting. The tomb was discovered in the 19th century by Secondiano Campanari. He named it after the queen Hosa, saying he had seen a figure that immediately disappeared. Although there is a great deal of skepticism concerning this painting, there have been cases in which the brusque changes in climate following the opening of a tomb caused the paintings there to disappear. Doubts obviously remain as to the attribution of the figure to the queen. It was in any account Dennis' narration which made the tomb, which seems to date to the Hellenistic period (4th-3rd cent. BC), famous throughout Europe.

There are twenty-six tunnels in this intricate rock-cut tomb, including the

main one (dromos) which leads into a larger room originally supported by two or three pillars. Other tunnels, still not completely dug out, run along on several levels, reaching a depth of a score or more meters underground and connecting the complex with the

exterior via two entrances at different levels. This type of gallery tomb is not unusual in Etruria and the most famous example is undoubtedly the Labyrinth of Porsenna in Chiusi. It has however recently been hypothesized that it was not actually a burial complex but rather a sacred site, in view of its central location with respect to the other monumental burials.

The Curunas Tombs

The three rock-cut tombs of the aristocratic Curunas family are located on the lowest of the three levels of the necropolis of the Madonna dell'Olivo, and mark a sort of private monumental site. They date to a period from the middle of the 4th century to the end of the 2nd century BC, as shown by the fine ensemble of sarcophagi now in the Museum in Tuscania. Despite the high rank of the owners, there seems to have been no particular decoration or distinguishing element on the exterior of these tombs.

Tomb of the Amazon Sarcophagus

This tomb, composed of two chambers which have partially collapsed, contained a sarcophagus with bas reliefs on all four sides, including an *Amazonomachy* (the sarcophagus is now in Room III of the Museo Archeologico in Tuscania). The fact that the cover was missing bears witness to previous violations of the tomb, located on the second of the three levels of the necropolis.

Necropolis of Calcarello

In this city of the dead the Campanari in 1839 found the tomb of the

This page and following page: *rock tombs in the necropoli of Tuscania.*

ry, civil offices held, etc.) or favorite myths and fables. The Etruscan tomb was a summary of life and thus the necropoli as a whole, in their structures, were cities of the dead, copies of the city of the living.

Necropolis of Peschiera

The discoveries of recent decades have made this cemetery one of the most significant ensembles of funerary architecture in inner southern Etruria dating to the archaic period (c 7th-6th cent. BC).

noble Vipinana family. The furnishings are now in the Archaeological Museum. The rock-cut tomb has no particular architectural elements except for its cube shape which projects from the tufa bank. The finds inside however were exceptional and the Campanari reproposed them in the copy of the tomb they built in their garden, in Piazza Basile, now the municipal garden.

friends and feasts (which is why the ensembles of vases are generally those used for mixing wine), references to games (through paintings or dice), frescoes of a sexual nature, or reliefs which depict the moments of major glory of the deceased (a victo-

In the valley of the Maschiolo, a stream that runs into the Marta River, two monumental tombs were discovered on the right bank. The real entrance on each facade led into a vestibule and three chambers, arranged in a cross in

Necropolis of Ara del Tufo

The necropolis of **Ara del Tufo** consists of archaic chamber tombs with gabled roofs, with funeral couches and decoration inside. These are house tombs in which the dwelling places of the living were reproduced for their eternal sojourn. For the Etruscans, life in the afterworld was not thought of as either better or worse than their life on earth, but rather a sort of oblivion, a non-being which they attempted to make less tragic by remembering the things that had been held dearest: the home, the family (this is why tombs were used for generations of burials), the depiction of banquets with

Monumental "die tomb" in the necropolis of the Peschiera.

one tomb, and on an axis in the other. A third "die-tomb" looks like a house with a gabled roof.

Tombs called 'of ogival section' have also come to light, as well as an example of an architectural facade and various moldings. There are however also later tombs.

Inside, and this holds true more or less for all the necropoli, large benches along the sides are divided into individual couches by a string course. The most important tombs include those, already mentioned, of the Statlana, Vipinana, Atna, and Curunas families (together with the Arinas, the Velna, Ceise and Velthuri they comprised the city's aristocracy). All these tombs, as well as the Grotta della Regina, built between the 4th and 3rd centuries BC,

remained partially in use up to the 1st century BC.

It is the archaic rock-cut gabled roof house tombs which make the necropolis of the Peschiera so important. Although limited in area and number, they represent an element that cannot be ignored in attempted reconstructions of contemporary domestic architecture. The layout of these tombs consists of three parallel rooms, with the central room serving as entrance vestibule to those at the sides. The facade is on one of the long sides and the level of the floor inside corresponds to that outside, features also to be found in tombs in other centers in Etruria (Blera, San Giuliano, Norchia, Castro). This type of tomb was first developed in Caere and then spread throughout inner Etruria, thanks in part to the presence of banks of tufa that were easy to excavate. The

structure of the roof however is new, and in the examples in Tuscania becomes considerably larger and more realistically executed than in other localities where the tombs are often fragmentary. These examples in Tuscania moreover seem to have gone beyond the original model, and reveal a development that is the fruit of a vital civic art panorama. The series of small house-shaped urns from Tuscania, in which the ashes of the deceased were kept, bears witness to this. The tombs with gabled roofs, as well as a portico, such as here in the necropolis of the Peschiera, can thus be looked upon as the most noteworthy expression of a funerary ideology which combines a careful search for exterior effects with the traditional carefully decorated tomb interior (new houses after death). In many cases the exteriors of the tombs give no hint of the wealth and care taken in the interior.

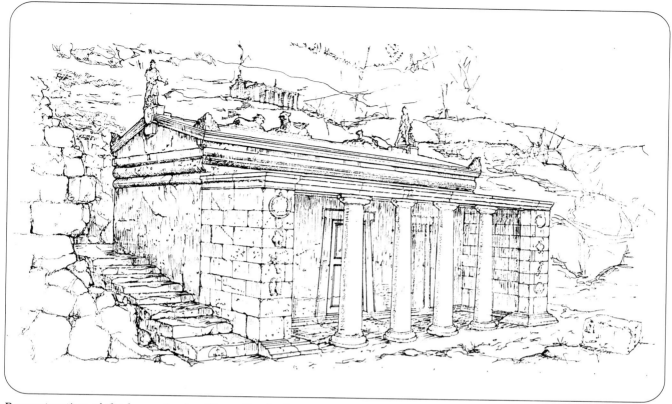

Reconstruction of the house tomb with portico in the necropolis of Pian di Mola (drawing by Virgilio Galati).

Probably these complexes were the result of different requirements. For the Etruscans their necropoli were more than simply cities of the dead, for sacred rites were celebrated throughout the year near the tombs (evidence of the sense of continuity of the relationship between the living and the dead). The funeral area was thus transformed into a large open-air sanctuary consisting of duplicates of real houses. The portico in front, as in the examples in Tuscania, would certainly have made it easier to celebrate these services.

Why this new type of Etruscan tomb in the shape of a house with a gabled roof and a portico should have been created is not known. The type spread to the major centers touched by the important inland communications route which radiated out from Tuscania and became the Via Clodia in Roman times. This is a clear indica-tion that in the archaic period the city was also important as an artistic center. The ornamentation would seem to suggest that influences from the principal centers of the region merged in the art workshops of the city. Sculpture fragments found near the Peschiera necropolis tombs recall the area of Vulci. The false doors and encased columns which decorate the die tombs on the other hand recall Tarquinia and the contemporary tombs of Castro. In addition to various decorative elements, which are unique to the archaic period, the great care bestowed on the execution of all architectural and ornamental details in the principal Tuscanese tombs seems to indicate a milieu that was quite avant-garde. Archaic Tuscania certainly played a leading role in the development of architecture (funerary, civil and religious) in the early Etruscan period.

Necropolis of Pian di Mola

The necropolis of Pian di Mola is situated on the left bank of the Maschiolo stream, across from the Peschiera necropolis. This highly important group of burials contains examples of tombs in line with those of the group across the way.

House tomb with portico

In 1984 a thick layer of earth brought down through the centuries by landslides was removed, leading to the discovery of this very important house tomb. All four sides stand free from the rock and the tomb has a gabled roof. As in the examples in the Peschiera necropolis, it was originally preceded by a portico, of which the Tuscan bases (two are worked in a single block) remain. Four columns, with screen walls in between, supported the flat roof of the portico, to which a staircase, next to one of the screen walls, led. This upper part of the portico certainly served for cult practices. The monument, on the basis of the materials which were found inside, even though in a fragmentary condition, (now in the Museo Archeologico Nazionale in Tuscania) and the stylistic characteristics has been dated to the second quarter of the 6th century BC, in other words the archaic period in Etruscan history.

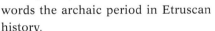

The **exterior** was therefore originally in the form of a portico set before a cube cut out of the tufa, in which the actual tombs were set. Traces of the portico can be seen on the ground, and the entrance door, which was closed by a large stone slab, is at the center of the main facade, on the long side. The short sides have triangular pediments and the gabled roof originally had decorative disk-shaped elements on top (there are some in the finds in the Museum). In shape and stylistic complexity they are, up to now, unique for the archaic period. Pedestals (known as acroteria) were also set on the top of the roof. They supported statues of divinities in nenfro. Some of these were found in the area in front of the entrance. The outer walls of the cube are carved in relief with moldings and cornices, closely related to the structural elements of the dwellings. It is interesting to note that the decorations on the short northern side are more summarily executed than those on the short southern side. Either the ornamentation of the tomb was interrupted at a certain point or hastily finished (or two different groups of workers might

have been employed, with those working on the south less skillful). The quality of the finds (outstanding in the Museum in Tuscania is a molding with a crouching *feline*) and the presence of the rows of pedestals on the roof for statues and images, would lead one to think that this was a monumental area, with particularly rich sepultures, within the entire necropolis.

The **interior** has a rather articulated ground plan with three funerary chambers set along the facade (N-S). The ones at the sides have a gabled ceiling with clearly visible exposed beams while the funerary benches below, on which the bodies were laid out and where the offerings accompanying the dead to the netherworld were placed, have cushions and footrests. The central chamber also served as vestibule. A ground plan of this sort could only have been closely connected with the dwellings in the Etruscan cities, and anticipated what the remains of Etruscan urban layouts of the second half of the 6th century (as in Acquarossa, one of the best known) have to tell us.

In 1984 another rock-cut sepulchral monument on the eastern ridge of the necropolis of Pian di Mola was identified and explored. It distinguishes itself for the originality of the layout and the decorative ensemble, an indication that there is still a great deal to be discovered in these necropoli.

The Museum, where installation is still in progress, houses funerary furnishings from Tuscania, distributed in the various rooms according to their discovery site. Finds from the necropolis of the Madonna dell'Olivo, the richest of all, and from Calcarello are in the rooms on the ground floor. Above are three other rooms with the more recent discoveries from the cemeteries of Pian di Mola, Ara del Tufo and Scalette.

GROUND FLOOR

Room I
Curunas Tombs I and III

*Curunas Sarcophagi
from the necropolis
of the Madonna dell'Olivo*

These extremely fine sarcophagi belonged to the Curunas family. The portraits of the deceased are typically Etruscan in their realism, and, unlike the Greek works, at least of the late period, have truly captured the expressive character of the deceased. This is not a 'realism' which aimed at a perfect beauty that was the sum of the main aesthetic values of the society, but an attempt to give the figure his true identity by expressing some unique aspect of

character or appearance. The juxtaposition of masses and lines which sometimes makes the Etruscan 'portrait' more angular, sharper and chiaroscuro than the classic portrait thus accentuated the essential features and physiognomic elements. The figures moreover almost always seem lost in thought, or even with a hint of a smile which has been frozen. They are participants in the banquet whose death has made their happy moments no more than a pale memory.

The bas reliefs on the front of the sarcophagi echo Hellenistic themes to be found in Etruscan art of the 4th century BC, including tritons (fish/men) engaged in battle or marine monsters. These sarcophagi in dark nenfro were once brightly painted and traces of color are still visible.

A museum case in the room contains a bronze bell-krater, a vessel in which wine was mixed with water before serving (the Greeks and the Etruscans never drank their wine straight during the banquets. This was something only drunkards did). This krater shows how rich the tomb furnishings of Curunas Tomb I were. The handle consists of a reclining female figure (like those on the sarcophagi), supported by two *tritons*, while the attachment plaque is decorated in relief with a figure lost in thought between two winged *genii* (mythical beings whose image was to continue on into Christian iconography as angels). The krater is dated to the late 4th century BC.

Preceding page, top to bottom: *interior of a die tomb with funerary couches; decorated handle of a bronze krater (Museo Archeologico Nazionale).*
Above: *sarcophagus of the Curunas family (Museo Archeologico Nazionale).*
Below: *view of the cloister.*

Room II
Curunas Tomb II

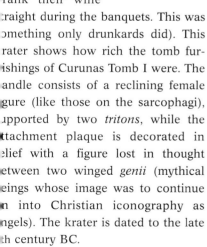

The rich furnishings of this tomb numbered almost five hundred pieces. This room contains only nine of the many sarcophagi found there, a funerary urn (with the bones and ashes of the deceased) and a cippus or marker set in memory of the deceased on the tomb which was used by various members of the family for more than a hundred years and thus contains materials belonging to different periods and styles. The oldest sarcophagi are those which show the figures lying down on the lid, even when holding the cup, or patera, in which wine was drunk (a sort of preparation for eternal sleep). The later ones show the deceased reclining on a triclinium, the couch used by the nobles (and later the Romans) during banquets and feasts. The showcase in the center contains objects which accompanied

Sarcophagus of the Curunas family, with tritons.

31

the deceased. To be noted are the bronze mirrors, on which mythological scenes and figures have been engraved *(Dioscuri, an assembly of gods)*, vases, in bronze, with handles in the form of female figures, good luck objects, oil lamps, various theater masks, a red-figure cup known as skyphos, imported from Attica, with *Dionysus and a satyr*, a scene which is related to the serving of wine and feasts centered on intoxication. The best products of Greek pottery were sent to the markets of Etruria, rich thanks to the presence of metal ore. The Etruscan elite, culturally more backward but economically very well off, adopted many traditions and customs from their Greek suppliers, such as the alphabet. What makes the Etruscan language "mysterious" is not an incapacity to decipher the words (which are actually quite easy to read) but the fact that few texts are available, limited mostly to a great quantity of tomb inscriptions (the problem therefore comes down to trying to reconstruct a civilization through tombstones, with a very limited vocabulary in this specific context).

Room III
Necropolis dell'Olivo and the discoveries of the Campanari Family

The room is dedicated to the find in the Necropolis of the Madonna dell'Olivo, one of the first to be investigated by the Campanari family in the first half of the nineteenth century. A few explanatory panels regarding the Campanari family are also included in the exhibition. At the center is the sarcophagus with bas-reliefs running around all four sides. Shown is an *Amazonomachy* or battle of the Amazons, a Greek myth adopted by the Etruscans. The Amazons were mythical female warriors who lived in a city commanded by a queen and when they were still children their right breasts were cut off so they could use the bow and sword better. Their kingdom may have been in Thrace, or the Caucasus, but Heracles went to Cappadocia to get the girdle that belonged to their queen Hippolyta (some have interpreted this as an allusion to the old Hittite kingdom in Anatolia, and the capital Hattusa, not far from Ankara). The traditional Near Eastern and later Greek scenes of the

Top to bottom: *bronze krater; bronze mirror (Museo Archeologico, Florence); red-figure skyphos with Dionysus and a satyr; theater masks.*

hunt and of fighting animals are not always shown. The protecting deity of the Amazons was Artemis, goddess of the hunt. In Etruria Amazon myths were always very popular because they corresponded to the active role of women in Etruscan society (later inherited by women in Rome).

The figures of *lions* in this room are in poor condition. Various other fragments include some, that like the very worn lion, may have come from Curunas Tomb III. Others may come from the Vipinana tomb, including a *lion with the head of a ram and a human head in his clutch*. This is a terror-inspiring depiction, frequently found in tombs, and sometimes meant to recall events that had really happened. More often however they reveal the anguish of an extremely transient human condition continuously threatened in life and then carried away in the vortex of an eternal night populated by monsters and demons (such as *Charu* and *Tuchulcha* on a vase from Tuscania that is now in Trieste). Medieval sculptors turned to the relief sculpture for inspiration.

Decorated sarcophagus (Museo Etrusco Gregoriano, Vatican City).
Center: *two-handled bowl, 15th century (Private collection, Viterbo).*
Below: *Etruscan sarcophagus in terra-cotta.*

Room IV
Vipinana Tomb
and the Necropolis
of Calcarello

In 1839 the Campanari discovered the tomb of the aristocratic Vipinana family in locality Calcarello. It was the wealth of this hypogeum burial, furnished with numerous sarcophagi, that inspired the antiquarians to set up their Campanari Garden, a few months later, in what is now Piazza Basile, near the Town Hall. The smaller elements in the ensemble – vases, urns, objects – dating to a long period from between the 4th to the 2nd century BC, were dispersed a few years after the creation of the Garden. There are now only twelve sarcophagi here (some of the total of twenty four are now in the Piazza del Comune). The one with the depiction of the *myth of the Danaïds* dating to the turn of the 4th century BC is of particular

note. The sarcophagus itself (the lid is missing) is carved with bas-reliefs on all four sides. One side shows the *Punishment of the Daughters of King Danaos*, ordered by their father to kill their husbands. On one short side is a *duel*; on the back is a *scene of sacrifice*; on the other short side is the *Sacrifice of Iphigenia*, sacrificed by her father as a result of the victory in the Trojan War.

UPPER FLOOR

Room I
Portico Tomb
in Pian di Mola

Finds from the portico tomb in the necropolis of Pian di Mola are on exhibit here. To be noted are a *disk shaped acroterium*, one of the decorative gable elements. It consists of a nenfro "nut" (attached to the roof) on which a disk, visible on the facade, and a small round pedestal were fastened with studs. The center hole or tenon for the mortise is visible.

Another decorative element was set on the small round pedestal. This type of decorative framing of the pediments is currently rather rare in archaeological Etruria but was more widespread in Campania where it appeared as early as the first half of the 6th century. Many other Etruscan tombs (and temples) must however have had this type of disk acroterium as evidenced by representations on mirrors, as well as votive urns.

The relief of a *feline* on a torus molding also comes from the same tomb. The molding is shaped on the back so that it could be embedded. This relief fell from the tomb after one of the various landslides, and was found nearby in 1984. The nenfro sculpture in the round of a crouching lion is of good quality even if some parts are missing. The subject is not new in the Etruscan funerary tradition, but the execution and the vitality of the animal make it a piece worthy of note. It has been pointed out that the attention paid to the characterization of the features (the tightly shut jaws, the large protruding eyes) must mean that the participants in the funeral ceremonies had a rather close-up view of the lion (might it have been set on the eaves of the portico in front of the actual burial cube structure?)

The relief of the *sphinx* also comes from the same tomb. Half of the body and the claws are missing. It was also a roof ornament. The porportions of this imaginary monster, whose iconography arrived in Etruria via eastern products, are graceful and carefully done. The hair style and treatment of the wings recall the artistic production of Vulci. However with respect to the materials from Vulci, the outright frontality of the figure, and the schematic quality of the braids which fall vertically on her shoulders, forming a rather compact structure, make this sphinx more rigid. This may mean that the relief is older than those from

Urn with dying Adonis (Museo Etrusco Gregoriano, Vatican City).

the Vulci workshops or that the more archaic and traditional features of Etruscan sculpture lingered on in Tuscania.

The relief of a *lion* also comes from the "house tomb with portico" in the necropolis of Pian di Mola. The piece has been recomposed, although it still looks very fragmentary. It was found, like the other acroteria statues (on the roof), in front of the portico that originally stood before the actual die tomb, and seems to be very carefully made. It also would seem to be close to materials from Vulci, which would set it into the second quarter of the 6th century BC (575-550 BC).

A *house-shaped cippus* was also found next to the portico in front of the tomb. It was however set over a shaft tomb dating to the 5th century BC. This time the representation of a real house was not used to create new rooms. Made to contain the ashes or bones of the deceased, the basic concept was the same.

Room II
Treptie Tomb
in Pian di Mola

Several sarcophagi covers in terracotta, rather than in nenfro, are on

exhibit in this room. They com from a series of sepulchers dat ing to the 3rd cent. BC, found i the tomb of the aristocrati Treptie family. To be noted th sarcophagus in the center, wit the figure of a lady decked ou in her jewelry, consisting c necklace, earrings and ha clasp, and wearing her fines dress for the funeral banque Her facial features have bee modeled with characteristi Etruscan realism (features then t appear in Roman folk art). She commonly identified as the *Mothe in-law*.

Room III
Tomb furnishings
from the
Orientalizing Period
(7th-6th cent. BC)

The tomb furnishings shown her date to the Orientalizing Period (7tl 6th cent. BC), when Etruscan art wa influenced by the fine metalwork pro duced in the cities of Ionian Greec or Phoenicia and the Assyrian an Cypriote wares imported by Greek Punic and Near Eastern merchant: as well as by the Etruscans them selves, to the Tyrrhenian coasts an inland, trading them with rich iro materials. These finds come from th necropoli of Ara del Tufo, Pian (Mola and Scalette. Of particular not is a frieze of brightly painted terra cotta slabs in low relief depicting banquet turned into an orgy by th fumes of wine. Sexuality in classi Antiquity and Etruria was much free before Christian morality, derive from the Hebrew mentality and tha of other Near Eastern peoples, wa introduced. Sex, from the religiou and moral point of view, was joyous the symbol of the fullness of life and health. In Etruscan tombs, in which the care-free aspects of life and the recreational activities the deceased once enjoyed were summed up, depictions of sexual activities of all types were common, including matrimonial, heterosexual, orgiastic (some of the favorite themes were those involving Dionysus and the satyrs), and homosexual love. The normality of the orgiastic type is highlighted in this relief by the association of the lovemaking scenes in the upper register with the genre scenes below where dogs are shown underneath the triclinia eating the remains of the banquet. To be noted on the right is the large krater for mixing wine, set on a tall pedestal with a double volute, once again a coupling of wine/eroticism.

The showcases contain objects in *bucchero*, the typical dark pottery of the Etruscans made to resemble metal objects. Some are decorated with geometric motifs. The production of b*ucchero* was characteristic of the earlier stages of the Etruscan civilization in Etruria. The Greeks themselves never produced these wares but imported them from Etruria. As the Etruscan sea-faring power spread throughout the Mediterranean area, so did *bucchero*. It was not a black glazed pottery (like the common ware of later centuries, and like the red or black-varnished *terrae sigillatae* of the Romans, which was perhaps a hangover from the older *bucchero* ware). These wares were made with special clay and the firing technique was such that the fabric of the vessel was gray or black and the outside had a metallic sheen.

Church and former convent of Santa Maria del Riposo
Via del Riposo

The zenith of Renaissance art in Tuscania is represented by the church of Santa Maria del Riposo, built in 1495 on a preceding church, traces of which remain in the large two-light window in the apse dating to the 13th-14th century. The works of art inside the church are stylistically in keeping with the church itself. They all date to the 15th and 16th centuries, ranging from the wooden *Crucifix,* to the frescoes and the panels by Scalabrino da Pistoia, the retable behind the high altar by Giulio Pierino d'Amelia [1543-1581, known as "Pierin del Vago" but not to be confused with the more famous Florentine painter Pietro Buonaccorsi known as "Pierin del Vaga", 1501-1547] and Pastura, to the *Presentation in the Temple* by Gerolamo Siciolante da Sermoneta, and the wooden choir stalls of 1534 [extensively restored after the 1971 earthquake].

The simple **facade** of the church has three imposing buttresses and an ornate portal in nenfro dating to 1532 as well as a large oculus in the upper tier. The fine feeling for space and the elegant lines are typically Tuscan.

The **interior** is spacious and full of light, with a nave and two aisles separated by columns. There is an interesting holy water font in nenfro dating to the 14th century at the entrance. Plaster that fell as a result of the earthquake revealed a late 16th century *Madonna and Child* on the right wall. A large wooden altarpiece, known as retable, carved and with paintings, is located on the high altar.

Facade of the church of Santa Maria del Riposo.

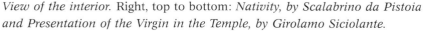

View of the interior. Right, top to bottom: *Nativity, by Scalabrino da Pistoia and Presentation of the Virgin in the Temple, by Girolamo Siciolante.*

A *Madonna and Child* by the Umbrian painter Antonio del Massaro known as Pastura (15th century) is set into the center of the retable.

After the activity of the painter Lorenzo da Viterbo, Pastura soon became known as one of the most important artists working in the area of Viterbo. His manner was the most esteemed variant in Lazio of the artistic idiom of Perugino and his workshop, thanks to his relaxed and comprehensible style. The production of Pastura's School in the Viterbo area however is still a moot question, involving works of the later 16th century as well, just because this idiom succeeded in adapting itself so well to a variety of requirements.

In the paintings of *St. John the Baptist* and *St. Francis* which frame Pastura's *Madonna*, Giulio Pierino d'Amelia still reflects proto-Renaissance stylistic features [probably to harmonize with the *Madonna*].

Madonna and Child (late 16th cent.). Right, top to bottom: *Saint Francis, detail of the altar piece by Giulio Pierino d'Amelia (now attributed to Maestro Pellegrino, 1516)* and *Madonna and Child by Pastura.*

More recent art historians however are loath to accept Faldi's attribution of the paintings at the sides of the polyptych to Giulio Pierino d'Amelia. They are thought to be the work of another artist active in the area who painted the *Nativity*, also in this church, as well as a triptych (in Santa Maria Maggiore in Tivoli) and the *St. Vincent Ferrer* in the Museo Civico in Viterbo. It does however seem to be an only slightly earlier painter, from the Roman ambience of Raphael, so much so that Pierin del Vaga, a student of Raphael's, has been proposed instead of Giulio Pierini, making the date of the painting earlier (might it not also be by Siciolante?).

The *St. Anne and the Presentation of Mary in the Temple* in the left aisle of the church is by Girolamo Siciolante (1521-1580).

This panel is practically the only evidence that the 16th century art world in Tuscania was aware of what was being done elsewhere, despite the fact that the painter was, significantly, the most conservative and old-fashioned painter in Raphael's following.

Siciolante represents the artistic trend that was particularly fond of the sweetness and soft passages of light and color to be found in Raphael's late works, chronologically between the 1550s and 1560s, a period in which the general tendency was for the chiaroscuro tones and brusque passages of Michelangelo's style. Many art historians therefore tend to consider

Siciolante as a rather conservative painter even though he belongs to the generation of artists of the "third phase" of Mannerist painting. He was called to Piacenza (1545-46) by Pier Luigi Farnese and then distinguished himself among the young artists called in by Paul II Farnese for the decoration of Castel Sant'Angelo (1547) in Rome, and subsequently, in 1553-54, for the decoration of the church of Sant'Andrea on the Via Flaminia (1551-1553), just finished by Iacopo Barozzi known as Vignola for the Pope. Siciolante's activity in Tuscania therefore comes as no surprise, considering the fact that Cardinal Gambara, also a member of the Farnese family, had bestowed various commissions in the city in the field of architecture, further evidence of the unity between the pictorial and the architectural milieus.

Above: *fresco with God the Father, Enthroned Madonna and Saints, in the left aisle.*
Above and following page, below: *details of the predella of the large altarpiece on the high altar, with the Nativity of*

A niche on the left aisle of the church contains a *Nativity*, also 16th century and perhaps attributable to Pierin del Vaga. Also to be noted are the three altarpieces, with the *Nativity*, the *Adoration of the Magi and the Shepherds*, and the *Deposition*, outstanding works by Scalabrino da Pistoia (1489-?). They underline the close cultural relationship between Tuscania and the entire Viterbo area, beginning in the second half of the 15th century, above all with Siena and Florence.

The principal archaeological remains in Tuscania itself include a portion of the Via Clodia and the so-called "Bagno della Regina" (Baths of the Queen), together with fragments of the old walls. These can be seen on the way to the basilica of San Pietro since these fragments of the oldest Tuscania are alongside the road leading to the medieval basilica.

the Virgin, *Presentation of the Virgin in the Temple; Marriage of the Virgin; Adoration of the Shepherds; Adoration of the Magi; Flight to Egypt*, by Maestro Pellegrino (16th cent.). Above: *Nativity*, in the left aisle (16th cent.).

Adoration of the Shepherds, by Scalabrino da Pistoia.

The sixteenth century reconstruction of the medieval fabric and the Campanari family

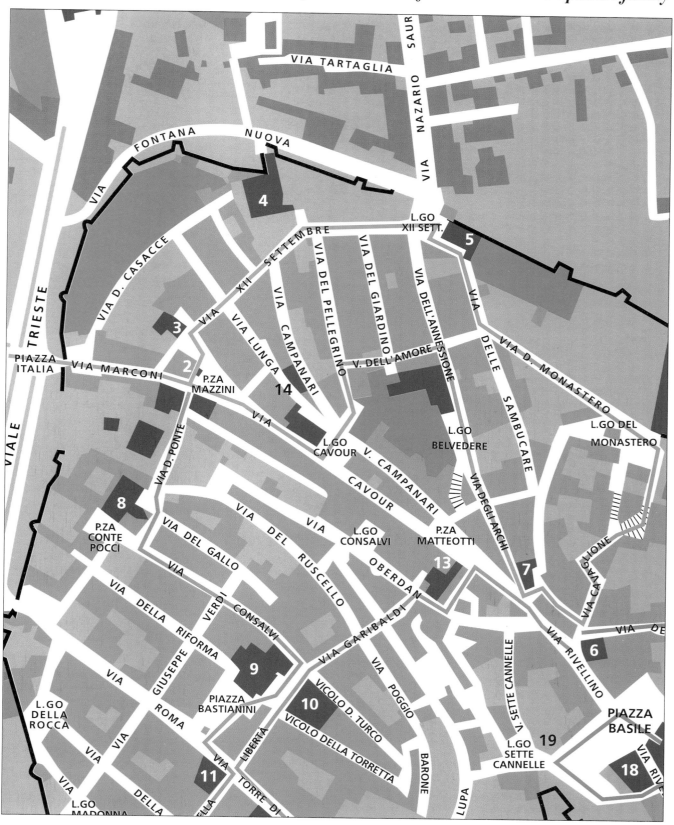

Although Tuscania has relatively little in the way of painting and even less movable sculpture, with the exception of what is in the two great basilicas, it can boast of two of the finest church buildings of medieval Italy: the basilicas of San Pietro and of Santa Maria Maggiore. One is located at the top, the other at the foot, of the highest hill in the city, in a secluded site, overlooking the country-side. Together

they are one of the most evocative and romantic ensembles imaginable. By comparison the other medieval churches in town reflect the diminishing political importance of the city and its economical regression. Unlike Viterbo and other medieval centers, no outstanding political or administrative buildings were left in Tuscania after the old Town Hall (the Rivellino) was destroyed. The best examples of urban architecture are a few dwelling houses. The unhurried visitor can discover a great deal on his own by wandering through the smaller streets and peering into the more hidden corners. In the steeply sloping Via degli Archi, the arches that cross over from one old house to another create a fascinating play of open areas and shady hollows, while the houses at the corners where two or more streets meet act as picturesque backdrops.

Via Marconi takes you to the core of the city itself.

The Montascide fountain
Largo Bixio/Piazza Mazzini

Although the Baroque period added little to the general features of the city, the Montascide fountain (1623 but renovated in the 18th century), [with waterspout masks] and surmounted by the municipal coat of arms, is typically Baroque in its turgid forms and theatrical approach.

Turn right into Via XII Settembre.

Church of San Marco
Via XII Settembre

Up until 1971 the only remaining part of its original Romanesque struc-ture was the portal.

Consecrated in 1333, the church was completely renovated in 1843. The portal in the facade, with small spiral columns, a 16th century *Madonna and Child* in the lunette and an octagonal oculus above, is all that is left of the original building. The closing up of the side door and the large arch overhead show that the original architectural organism was quite different from what we see today and that the Romanesque portal itself was set into an earlier building. Consolidation works after the 1971 earthquake were carried out with an eye to 'liberating' the building and restoring its presumed medieval appearance, despite the fact that it had already been considerably modified by the additions of later centuries. It would probably not have been opportune to rebuild the 19th century decorative ensembles which fell in the quake, just as it would have been impossible to reproduce the

Romanesque portal of the church of San Marco.
Above: *Montascide fountain.*

various strata added throughout the centuries. In the **interior** however the removal of all later layers of plaster has completely uncovered the great Gothic pointed arches, which had been revealed by the quake. The open timber truss roof, supported by the arches, also plays a part in turning the space into a picture of 'twentieth century' Umbrian Gothic. Subsequent detachment of later layers of plaster also revealed the presence of 14th century frescoes, including an *Annunciation* and a *Madonna and Child* in a niche to the left of the inner facade, with a *God the Father and Angels* up above. These fragments, together with discoveries in other city churches, present us with varied aspects and greatly enrich the panorama of painting in Tuscania in the 14th and 15th centuries. A wooden 15th century *Cross* from the church of Santa Maria del Riposo is behind the high altar. This is one of the few surviving fine wooden

Fourteenth century fresco of the Annunciation.
Above: *facade of the church of San Marco.*

Fourteenth century fresco in the intrados with a bishop.

Madonna and Child, fourteenth century fresco (intrados).

Wooden 15th century Crucifix.

furnishings of the many that once adorned the sacred places in the city, together with painted panels and frescoes.

Continuing along Via XII Settembre, and down a few steps, one reaches the Piazzale della Madonna della Rosa.

Blessing Christ, on the intrados keystone.

Church of
Santa Maria della Rosa

Piazzale della Madonna della Rosa

When the area around the hill of San Pietro was depopulated after the sack of 1495, this church became the cathedral.

The **exterior** reflects Romanesque-Gothic forms, without any particular stylistic element on the facade, which is characterized by its horizontality.

This is emphasized by the two protruding string courses which divide the facade into tiers. The front is in nenfro, the typical local stone of volcanic origin. This volcanism is still present in the form of hydrothermal springs and is responsible for the tremors which occasionally make themselves felt in the area. Nenfro is a tufaceous stone that is light and easy to work (but not

Assumption of the Virgin and Saints.

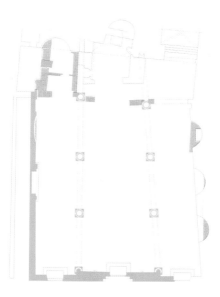

carve: which explains the coarseness of the reliefs) and relatively durable. In the course of centuries this facade was modified various times, as revealed by the break in the lower cornice and

signs of two openings which were later filled in. When the 1971 quake struck, restoration had just been completed with "the elimination of two false two-light windows on the facade" (Pacini),

Church of Santa Maria della Rosa.

Apse area. Right, top to bottom: *columns with fresco remains with St. John the Baptist and detail of the Madonna and Child with St. Peter and St. Secondianus, in the apse.*

while inside what was left of a chapel built for the vestiges of an image of the *Madonna* originally painted over the arch of one of the city gates was brought to light. The arch had subsequently been incorporated in the church structure.

The **interior,** which is 15th century in its present state, is charac-

terized by a singular asymmetry.

The nave and two aisles, revealed on the facade by the variation in the projection of the sections of the building, are separated by eight columns from which round-headed arches spring. Here too, work carried out after the 1971 quake was done with a view to restoring the presumed

medieval aspect of the building to th detriment of what subsequent cen turies had added. For example th apse part was rediscovered and mad visible, while other structures wer carried out in a decidedly neo medieval style. A series of previousl unknown frescoes also came to ligh when the plaster fell off. They wer part of the rich decoration which, her

Side aisle.
Above: *interior.*
Right: *Panel with the Madonna of the Rosary.*

too, once covered the walls of the building (in particular a 13th century *Madonna and Child between Saints Peter and Secondianus* in the apse).

A fresco of the *Madonna and Child*, known as the *Madonna lib-*

eratrice or *Madonna of Salvation*, is connected to the ferocious destruction of the city in 1495 by the troops of Charles VIII. The sudden outbreak of a storm that ended the plundering is attributed to the intercession of the Madonna. (Legends of this kind find comparison with similar images in other churches in the area, such as that of *Santa Maria Santissima liberatrice* in the church of the Trinità in Viterbo, said to have saved the city from a natural catastrophe in 1320).

Continuing along Via XII Settembre up to Largo XII Settembre.

Church of San Silvestro
Largo XII Settembre

The building was founded in the 14th century and has a simple portal with spiral columns and a

Church of San Silvestro

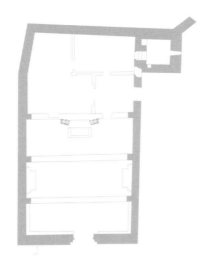

bell tower with one level of two-light openings. Inside is a fresco of the *Tree of Jesse* from the early 14th century. It has been attributed [for the time being] to Gregorio and Donato d'Arezzo, who also did the surviving paintings in the church of Santa Maria Maggiore.

Recently it seems more likely that the subject matter of the fresco is not the *Tree of Jesse*, but the *Tree of the Cross* as described by Saint Buonaventure.

Other frescoes emerged after the

Church of San Silvestro.
Above: *fresco of the Crucifixion in the intrados of the third arch.*

Fresco of the Tree of Jesse (or Tree of the Cross).
Below: *entrance of Palazzo Spagnoli.*

quake of 1971 and the detachment of later frescoes. Among these is a *Crucifixion* in the intrados of the third arch, an indication that originally most of the church was frescoed, a sign of the flourishing economy of the time in the city.

Continuing along Via del Monastero leads to Largo del Monastero (with the large monastery of San Paolo) and then on along Via Cavaglione.

Palazzetto Farnese
Via Cavaglione/corner Via Rivellino

This small Renaissance palace has a Guelph cross window and an external overhanging staircase (*profferlo*) decorated with barbicans.

The coat of arms of the Farnese family is over the portal. The *profferlo* (from the Greek: "ro" and "fero", that

is 'brought forward') is an architectural structure particularly common in the area of Viterbo. The houses generally had warehouses or stables on the ground floor and this steep external staircase with a landing or terrace at the top in front of the main entrance solved the problem of how to reach the official living quarters on the first level.

On the other side of the street is a medieval tower, its top cut down, an example of the old tower houses of Tuscania which were destroyed by the artillery of Charles VIII and never rebuilt.

Go along Via Rivellino, towards the right, until you come, on your right, to Via degli Archi.

Palazzo Spagnoli
Via Rivellino/Via Valle dell'Oro
Via degli Archi

This 14th century palazzo, also

known as the "Profferlo degli Spagnoli" has a typical *profferlo* or outside staircase and a Romanesque-Gothic two-light window.

The 14th century Gothic two-light

Above and following page: *Via degli Archi.*

window consists of two pointed arches, filled in at the top by polylobate stone tracery, and with a small column with elongated leaves on the capital in between.

Continue along Via dell'Annessione/Via dell'Amore/Via Pellegrino on the left/Via Campanari on the right.

Dwelling house
Via Campanari

This 13th century house has a low overhang and Gothic one-light windows, and with walls as thick as those of a fortress.

Former Palazzo Campanari and Campanari Garden

Via Campanari
Contrada della Cava

The garden of the former Palazzo Campanari is currently badly neglected, despite its considerable historical importance.

The Campanari family, from Tusca-

Medieval house in Via Campanari.
Above: *"profferlo" of Palazzo Spagnoli.*
Following page: *drawing of the interior of the tumulus in the Campanari Garden (Ainsley, 1842).*

nia, owned vast lands in the area of Tuscania and Vulci. They were the leading figures – as narrated by the English author George Dennis – in the first systematic excavations of the Etruscan necropoli in the area and in the sale, abroad, of a great number of the finds. They did not illegally plunder

the necropoli for what they did was a legal acquisition of materials found in their lands, much of which they were permitted to dispose of as they saw fit in line with the papal law of the time. The family fortunes then were tied to a cultural climate to be found throughout Europe, from Russia to

England, Sweden to Italy, characterized by the spread, between the 18th and 19th centuries, of a taste for historical periods (neo-Egyptian, neo-Greek, neo-Roman and even neo-Etruscan). Finds from the classical civilizations were in continuous demand and served as inspiration for new creations (such as the famous Wedgwood wares of the 18th century or of Sèvres or Prussia, made to imitate antique originals).

The Campanari, in addition to selling and finding objects also set up a carefully orchestrated system for the promotion of their products, bringing Tuscania to the limelight in Europe. In 1836-37 they inaugurated an exhibition of Etruscan and Greek objects in Pall Mall in London, with reconstructions of Etruscan tombs, to give the public an idea of the context in which their objects had been found. It was an important museum event and was already acknowledged as such by their contemporaries. This was when many European museums were opening Etruscan Rooms with materials that were actually mostly Greek, for ideas at the time as to what was Greek and what was Etruscan were still rather vague. In the reconstructions presented in the London show in Pall Mall, five of the eleven burial chambers shown were from Tuscania and were complete with their sarcophagi. Particularly striking was the reconstruction of a tomb in Tuscania where the four painted sarcophagi were accompanied by fifty or so vases and objects, mostly attached to the walls as they would have been in daily life (to put across the Etruscan con-

cept of tomb/house). The contents of the tombs was bought by the British Museum (which therefore has a great deal of material from Tuscania). It was this exhibition which stimulated Dennis to travel to ancient Etruria (before 1842), accompanied by Samuel James Ainsley who was charged with sketching the tombs described by Dennis. The results of this joint venture were some of the most fascinating views of Etruria and Tuscania ever made.

The London exhibition therefore launched the Campanaris into the European art world not only as the discoverers and merchants of Etruscan material, but also as exhibition curators, who could 'reconstruct' the ancient contexts. Shortly thereafter they also furnished indications for the imitation of a tomb, complete with furnishings, for the Museo Gregoriano

Etrusco in Rome. But the Campanari also formed a collection of their own, sadly no longer intact. In 1839, after the discovery of the Vipinana tomb, they installed the most "bizarre" Etruscan museum of all times in the courtyard-garden of their palace in Tuscania. Unfortunately this museum 'gem' has not come down to us. It consisted of cippi, sculpture, vases freely scattered around the garden, in informal ruins which formed a picturesque

Campanari Garden

setting for the reconstruction of the Vipinana die tomb. Inside the tumulus the antique dealers had placed most of the sarcophagi and furnishings originally there. In addition to various characteristic views of Tuscania, some of Ainsley's drawings now in the British Museum in London or published in Dennis' work also bear witness to this romantic historically oriented garden as well as to the reconstructed interior of the tumulus. It is indeed an example of a particularly evocative museum, but more than that of great inventiveness. The idea of an archaeological museum, part inside and part in the open air, such as the Campanaris had set up in Tuscania, was adopted in the garden of the Archaeological Museum of Florence almost a century later.

Campanari's achievements are therefore a prime example of 19th century collecting and museum installation which accompanied the reorganization of this part of Tuscania. Their work could be considered complete

when the two volumes of studies and surveys (including the medieval monuments) drawn up by Secondiano Campanari and which contributed greatly to the systematic studies of Tuscania and its history were published in 1855 and 1856. What the Campanaris did must be seen within its historical moment and should not be judged by later scientific parameters of archaeology. Their interests were first and foremost cognitive and of an antiquarian nature, certainly not scientific and interested in preservation, as one would expect them to be now.

Continue along Largo Cavour/Via Cavour and towards Piazza Mazzini.

Installations in the Campanari Garden (Ainsley, 1842).
Above: *tower-house on the corner where two streets meet.*

The sixteenth century grid
(Turn into Via Ponte and continue to Piazza Conte Pocci)

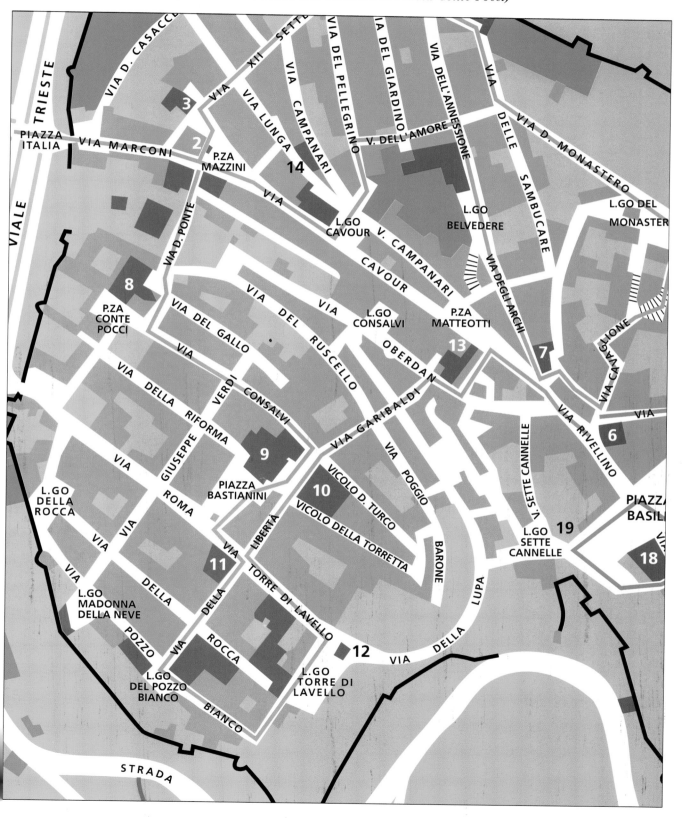

Crucifixion, fresco of Viterbo school, 15th century.

Church of Sant'Agostino
Piazza Conte Enrico Pocci

The church was built in the 14th century, but is important stylistically because of the Renaissance Ludovisi Chapel and the solemn arch decorated with bas-reliefs dedicated to Saint Job and dating to 1486, the fresco with the *Crucifixion* by a 15th century Viterbo painter and the tabernacle of the same date. The panel with the *Mother of Mercy* (now in the cathedral of San Giacomo) was originally in this church. It was thought to be by an unknown 15th century painter and is one of the few surviving examples of local 15th century figurative art. The stylistic idiom here too is close to Tuscan modes, especially in the light of the work of Benozzo Gozzoli and of Sassetta. The picture is characterized by a sophisticated amalgam of elements of local culture with those of the Tuscan culture between Siena and Florence (for a more thorough analysis see the Cathedral of San Giacomo).

The **interior** of the church consists of a nave only. After the quake of 1971, which damaged the 18th century decorations on the walls of the building (such as the stucco altar), fragments of the earlier 15th century decoration came to light, particularly in the apse.

An imposing Renaissance stone arch bearing reliefs with *Stories of Saint Job* and dating to 1486 is at the center of the right wall. The rich decoration, carved in nenfro, has been referred to the Sienese school of the second half of the 15th century with Andrea Bregno as one of the principal artists (Bregno sent reliefs for Cardinal Francesco Piccolomini's altar in the Cathedral in Siena from the papal court in Rome). Features of Bregno's art are to be seen particularly in the frieze of cherubs and garlands, while in the reliefs on the candelabra (that is the pilaster shafts), the sculptural idiom seems to be more antiquated. Scholars have therefore suggested that the sculptor responsible for this fine decoration might be a Sienese from the workshop of Antonio Federighi who was in the habit, at the time, of mixing various decorative features and spreading them from Siena to other towns in the Sienese *contado* or in the neighborhood.

The arch leads into the Ludovisi Chapel, with a fresco of the *Crucifixion*, dating to the early 15th century, in the apse. The tabernacle belongs to the final years of the 15th century, as does the frame around the fresco. The chapel was built in 1486, as mentioned in the inscription on the front of the arch, commissioned by the noble Paolo Ludovisi Toscanelli, lawyer for the Apostolic Secretariat.

The convent cloister too has an interesting Renaissance appearance.

Via Consalvi then leads to Piazza Bastianini or del Duomo.

Piazza and fountain of San Giacomo

The Baroque added little to the overall aspect of the city since this rich theatrical idiom was foreign to the local traditions, as was the case throughout the region of Viterbo. The simple 17th century fountain of San Giacomo (1621) still reflects the style of Vignola or Della Porta, and is attributed to Domenico Castelli.

Even though chronologically it is close to the Montascide fountain (which dates to 1623, renovated in the 18th century), these two works belong to completely different artistic currents. The fountain of San Giacomo may go back to a project of several decades earlier, part of the urban and architectural renewal program promoted by Cardinal Gambara, together with the facade of the Cathedral across the way. This project may then

have been taken up anew, perhaps by the architect himself (when Odoardo Farnese was cardinal?). The construction of Palazzo Giannotti, the principal noble palace in Tuscania, in the immediate vicinity of the Piazza, also stressed the centrality of the new Farnese installations in the sphere of the local notables.

Cathedral of San Giacomo

The clear-cut 16th century facade of the cathedral, a Renaissance work [1572], was built for Cardinal Giovan Francesco Gambara, and is unrelated to the inner structure [preexistent and later renovated]. It is almost the twin of the facade of the cathedral of San Lorenzo in Viterbo, which the same cardinal, bishop of Viterbo and Tuscania, had commissioned,

Cathedral of San Giacomo.
Above: *fountain in Piazza di San Giacomo.*

Predella panels from the polyptych by Andrea di Bartolo. Left to right: Last Supper, Kiss of Judas and Way to Calvary.

between 1560 and 1570 [more precisely between 1566 and 1576].

Piazza del Duomo, situated halfway between the old medieval fabric and the new 16th century urban grid, is of particular interest, particularly if seen in relation to the urban renewal policies Cardinal Alessandro Farnese promoted for many towns in Lazio. They often focussed on the construction of a large official building. Cardinal Giovan Francesco Gambara, bishop of Viterbo and Tuscania, was particularly involved in the territorial policies of the Farnese entourage.

Enthroned Madonna and Child with Saints, by Andrea di Bartolo.

Predella panels from the polyptych by Andrea di Bartolo. Left to right: Deposition from the Cross, Deposition in the Tomb, Resurrection. Below: *Crucifixion.*

The architect Giacomo Barozzi known as Vignola worked both for Gambara (in his villa of Bagnaia) and, more specifically, for Cardinal Farnese. Suggestions on the part of Vignola or his school are therefore not to be completely excluded for what was done in Piazza Duomo in Tuscania, with the facade of the new Cathedral of San Giacomo and then the foun-

tain. The same holds true for the Bishop's seat in Viterbo. In any case the cathedral was moved to the site of the old church of San Giacomo in 1572, and the new renovated building was consecrated in 1622.

The **facade** of the building stands as a sober backdrop, with a clear-cut alternation of plastered areas and dark architectural elements in nenfro. In size it contrasts sharply with the adjacent buildings, although the architectural idiom is not at all exuberant. This

is in keeping with a trend for simplicity, almost a rigorous poverty of style, common in the Counter-Reformation ambience of the Farnese milieu. The pilaster strips are very flat and slender in the lower Doric order tier while the pilaster strips above are of the Ionic order (a canonic superposition of the orders). The decorative elements are limited to the inscription celebrating the patron in the frieze ("H.JO.FRANC.CARD.DE GAMBARA EPISC. THUSCANEN.") and the small pilasters which support candlesticks at the corners. These small pilasters frame sweeping volutes which in turn connect the height of

the nave, marked at the top by a pediment, to that of the aisles. The principal portal, in comparison to the two side portals, shoots upwards. The 'conquests' of the Farnese architectural culture in the last decades of the 16th century, whose greatest architects were Vignola and Della Porta, therefore also come to Tuscania with a use of architectural elements which brings to mind the disputes regarding the facade of the church of the Gesù in Rome, also commissioned by Cardinal Alessandro Farnese. The rebuilding of San Giacomo, the old church of Tuscania, was financed by Gambara as well as by the City, which wanted a religious center that was more dignified than the cathedral of Santa Maria della Rosa.

The **interior**, on a basilica plan with a nave and two aisles, adopts a traditional ground plan, common in

Tuscania, which became fashionable in Counter-Reformation architecture of the second half of the 16th century with the spread in the *contado*, of the renewed Roman standard types.

Numerous works of art from various city churches are housed in the Cathedral, brought here to enrich the furnishings of the new building.

The 15th century polyptych with the *Madonna and Child with Saints*, by the Sienese painter Andrea di Bartolo (1389-1428), was originally in the church of San Francesco. It was a specifically local commission as shown by the presence at the feet of the *Madonna* of *messer Loccio* "toscanese" in the dress of the Apostolic Secretary.

The predella panels, also by Andrea di Bartolo, depict the *Last Supper*, the *Kiss of Judas, Way to Calvary,* the *Crucifixion,* the *Deposition from the Cross*, the *Deposition in the Tomb*, and the *Resurrection*. This is altogether one of the outstanding works of the period and reveals the adhesion and interest in the cultural world of Tuscania for Tuscan art, probably because that was where the patron came from.

The church also contains figures of *Saints* in niches, respectively of *St. Vito, St. Monica, St. Jerome, St. Augustine, St. Gregory the Great* and *St. Leonard.* They came here from the convent of San Giusto, five kilometers outside the city and now in

Top to bottom: *St. Vito (or St. Roch) and St. Leonard.*

Fifteenth century tabernacle.

ruins. The figures, recognized as "true masterpieces of the soave 15th century art" (Aureli), must originally have been part of an imposing altarpiece, given their size (a large retable above the altar table, probably with the figures in two tiers on either side of a central image which might have been either painted, or even the tabernacle attributed to Isaia da Pisa, now in the Cathedral and also from San Giusto). The *Saints* are set in early 16th century shell niches, unquestionably later than the statues themselves. The artistic idiom of the figures is strictly Tuscan in nature and dates to a few decades earlier (particularly in touch with the calligraphic line of the mid 15th century Florentine, Agostino di Duccio, as shown in the hair and beards,) and renewed in Lazio by Federico di Ubaldo da Firenze as late as 1509-1512, a demonstration of the persistence of this 'fashion'. These statues would in any case be datable to within the 15th century.

Also to be noted in the cathedral is the tabernacle with *Angels Holding Drapery Aside* to show the niche, used for the holy oil but originally meant for the preservation of the host. The relief has been attributed by Riccoboni to Isaia da Pisa. It comes from the convent of San Giusto and was recomposed from several fragments in 1981. There are also traces in the sculpture however, which has been defined as of "Sansovinian type", of features which would be archaic for the second half of the 15th century. Examples are the motif of the baldachin drapery and a certain hardness in the treatment of the figures. It is not a tabernacle in the latest Florentine style of the Rossellino, but closer in style to the work of Luca Della Robbia in Florence (Peretola) between 1441-43. There are abundant references to the antiquarian interests of Tuscan sculpture. Examples are the garlands and balusters

(wavy columns) at the side covered with acanthus leaves and framing the scene, while the position of the angels, the use of drapery and the archaic diadems on the heads of the *Angels*, still seem bound to late Gothic forms. But this was also the sculptural vocabulary used by outstanding sculptors such as Donatello and his partner Michelozzo. All this would make this example from Tuscania, if it were dated to the 1440s and not the end of the century, particularly up to date rather than antiquated. Nor is it chance that there is a companion to this tabernacle in the Museo Civico in Viterbo: two similar works for the two seats of the same Bishopric, in a sort of duplication of the church symbols. If however this example in Tuscania were to be dated to the 1470s, a sort of 'hangover' of Florentine culture of the 1440s, it could be seen in relation to the marble baptismal font of around 1471 by Francesco d'Ancona and Geronimo da Firenze for the cathedral of Viterbo.

Other works of importance in the Cathedral of San Giacomo are a *St. Bernardino and two Angels* by Sano di Pietro, still another example of the diffusion of Sienese art in Tuscania in the 15th century.

The two-sided triptych with the *Blessing Christ between Mary and St. John*, by Francesco d'Antonio Zacchi known as Balletta (1430-1476), was in Santa Maria Maggiore. The work, of the school of Viterbo, is

closely tied with the traditional iconography of the Savior, common in Lazio since it was bound to ancient rites. Signs of the painter's Tuscan and specifically Sienese artistic sources are however still evident.

On the main side of this triptych shaped panel, Balletta painted the *Blessing Redeemer between the Madonna and*

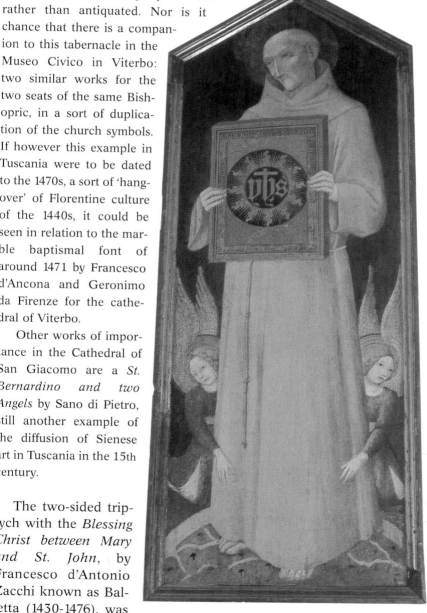

St. Bernardino, by Sano di Pietro.

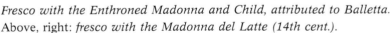

Fresco with the Enthroned Madonna and Child, attributed to Balletta.
Above, right: *fresco with the Madonna del Latte (14th cent.).*

Fresco with the Enthroned Madonna and Child (15th cent.).

St. John the Evangelist in tempera as well as the *Paschal Lamb* in the gable of the central compartment. On the back is the *Praying Madonna between St. John the Baptist and St. Cristina*, with a *cherub* and two *angels* in the gable. The work was attributed to Balletta on the basis of style (the work is not signed or dated) for the first time in 1925, and this attribution still seems to be accepted. On the whole the style was rather behind the times for the period in which it was painted. This brought the work close to influences of the Sienese masters as well as the persistence of a traditional iconography in the figure of the Redeemer which was still deeply felt in Roman Tuscia. The Sienese features to be seen in Balletta's work of the early 15th century clearly come to the fore in the dry handling of the profiles, the deeply indented Gothic drapery, the figure of the *Virgin* enclosed in a mandorla (on the back). There was a penchant for the International Gothic of nearby Siena which explains the presence in Tuscania of Sano di Pietro's *St. Bernardino* and above all, the polyptych with the *Madonna and Saints* by Andrea Bartolo.

Another work of importance is the fresco of the *Enthroned Madonna and Child.* It was detached after the 1971 quake since serious problems connected with its conservation were evident. Much of the color variations which gave the figures their volume had already fallen off. In 1972, after

Assumption of the Virgin, fresco of Sienese school (14th cent.).
Above, right: Mother of Mercy (15th cent.).

restoration and analysis, the work was attributed to Francesco d'Antonio Zacchi known as Balletta, who worked in Tuscania, above all because of the magnificent throne on which the *Virgin* is seated and the deliberate gesture of the *Child* with His finger in His mouth.

The panel known as the *Madonna dei Raccomandati* or *Mother of Mercy*, with the Madonna painted in tempera on the front (recto) and with the figure of *St. Nicholas of Tolentino* on the back (verso) was formerly in Sant' Agostino. It was formerly attributed to the 14th century, or to 15th century International Gothic school, influenced to a certain extent by Sassetta. Post-earthquake restoration however revealed an inscription in Gothic characters which made it possible to identify the painter and the patron. It seems to have been painted by Valentino Pica the Elder (1415-1490) from Viterbo, active around the middle of the 15th century, for Brother Pietro.

All other works by Pica, who was one of the favorite pupils of the more famous Balletta, have been lost. This panel therefore is one of the few certain examples of mid 15th century painting in Viterbo. Since Nicholas of Tolentino was canonized in 1446, it is probable that this work was commissioned a few years later to celebrate the event. In this case too, as in works by Balletta, figurative reference is still to the Sienese culture, in the decided abstraction of the figures, in the preciosity of the details, in the presence of singular realistic features (such as the bodies lying below).

Next to the church is the Bishop's palace, built in 1588 for Ludovico Carlo Montogli, the bishop who succeeded Giovan Francesco Gambara.

Lavello Tower.

Palazzo Giannotti
Piazza del Duomo

This imposing late 16th century building is one of the principal palaces in the city.

Palazzo Fani-Ciotti
Via Torre di Lavello
Via della Libertà

This 16th century building has an inner courtyard with portico and loggia.

Via della Libertà, Via Pozzo Bianco on the left/Largo Torre di Lavello.

Lavello Tower
Largo Torre di Lavello

This is one of the few surviving towers of medieval Tuscania (the one on the Palazzo del Bargello collapsed in 1954) and was built in the 15th century, by the lord of Tuscania, Angelo Tartaglia, right next to the Palazzo della Dogana, a dwelling house. All that remains today are a few two-light openings and the tower-entrance of Lavello incorporated into later buildings, as well as the coat of arms on the facade. This coat of arms has been quartered with that of the City and consists of a rampant griffin terminating in two volutes joined in a wheel. A similar coat of arms, once more of Tartaglia, was also to be found, according to Campanari, in the church of Santa Maria della Rosa. Halls and large subterranean premises which were part of the defensive system are still present on the lower floors. The palazzo was destroyed in 1421 when Tartaglia, who controlled most of the area of Viterbo and had been trying for seven years to establish an autonomous Seignoria over Tuscania, was abandoned by the Church and beheaded after his capture at Aversa. In March 1422 Pope Martin V granted full amnesty to the citizens of Tuscania and permission to take over the Tartaglia property. The plundering of his residence became a sort of sign of allegiance to new papal power and the palace, which had been a sort of autonomous castle within the city, was destroyed.

Along Via Torre di Lavello/Via della Libertà on the right/Piazza Duomo and Via Garibaldi up to Piazza Matteotti.

Small church of San Giovanni Decollato
Piazza Matteotti

This small building has a simple facade characterized by an octagonal wheel window (like the one in San Marco).

There was once a 17th century painting of the school of Caravaggio depicting the *Beheading of St. John the Baptist* inside. It was one of the few examples of cultural renewal in the milieu of Tuscania compared with the artistic conquests which had taken place in Rome several decades earlier.

Church of San Giovanni Decollato.

The Medieval vestiges
(From Piazza Matteotti turn into Via del Rivellino/then Via della Pace as far as Largo della Pace)

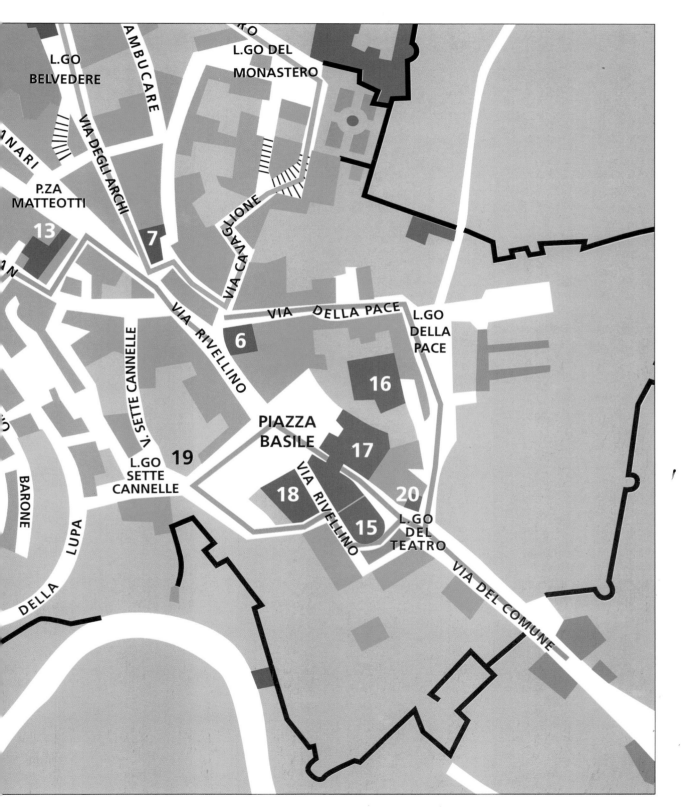

Gothic chapel in San Francesco: wall frescoed by Giovanni and Antonio Sparapane da Norcia. Below: St. Augustine, detail of a vault section.

Chapel in San Francesco, detail of the fresco.

Former church of San Francesco
Largo della Pace

The church and convent of San Francesco must have been particularly important among the monastic monuments of medieval Tuscania. The complex has long been de-consecrated and semi-demolished and used for other things but the imposing remains and their size, as well as the fact that some of the most important paintings of the city originally came from here, bear witness to what it once was. The polyptych with the *Madonna and Child* and the small panels with the *Story of the Passion of Christ* by Andrea di Bartolo were once here. Only the charming frescoes by Giovanni and Antonio Sparapane da Norcia, dating to 1466, still remain in the Gothic chapel. De-consecrated in the 19th century, torn down in large part and finally used as the municipal slaughter house, the church of San Francesco is today a superb stump, a symbol of the devastation of the cultural patrimony of the city that continued almost up to the present. In 1466 Giovanni and Antonio Sparapane signed and dated some of the fresco paintings in the vault and on the walls of the church. This is an important cycle of paintings in Late International Gothic style, with scenes of the *Crucifixion*, the *Last Judgement*, the *Doctors of the Church and Saints*. This refined culture, far from the lucid and exclusive Renaissance ideology of the large style-setting centers, was still the artistic idiom that characterized the smaller towns and the *contado*.

Continue up to Largo del Teatro.

Municipal Theater

The present Municipal Theater is recent structure, built after the dama inflicted by the collapse of the o Bargello tower in 1954 had be cleared away. Although it had fr quently been renovated, it was still t only surviving tower of the mediev Palazzo del Podestà.

Moving back along Via Rivellin pass under the large archway and to Piazza del Comune, or Piaz Basile on the Rivellino hill, fortified the Communal Period. This part of t city remained untouched by the 16 century settlement, and was n rearranged until the 19th century.

Former church of Santa Croce Municipal Library

The church of Santa Croce, prob bly dating to the 12th century but no de-consecrated, houses the Historic Archives and the Municipal Libra There are nine Etruscan sarcophagi the garden in front. The Campana had put a series of sarcophagi th

Town Hall, main facade. Below: *view of Tuscania, fresco inside the Town Hall.*

owned in the garden of the Hospital of Santa Croce, and also on a lot near San Francesco. The whereabouts of the real Campanari Garden (in the street of the same name) was forgotten and in the *Touring Club* guide of 1924 the area in front of Santa Croce was given as the garden of the antiquarians, an erroneous identification still in vogue.

Ruins of the Rivellino.

Palazzo Comunale (Town Hall)
(part of the complex of the former Rivellino)

On the left next to the underpass is the Town Hall (inside there are some Roman and medieval inscriptions), which was built on the site of the old Town Hall of the Bargello or the Podestà in the Rivellino complex, which was then torn down (the last tower collapsed in 1954 on the municipal theater). The messengers sent by Pope Boniface VIII to request the submission of the city seem to have been thrown out of the windows of the Rivellino Palace by the irate Tuscanesi.

Church of San Lorenzo or of the Holy Martyrs (SS. Martiri)
Piazza Basile

The church of San Lorenzo, or of the Holy Martyrs, is on the left. The first founding goes way back in time, although the present building is the result of the complete reconstruction of 1829.

The facade of the earlier church (prior to 1344) is still there on the left side. In the 19th century rebuilding the orientation of the church was changed.

Up until the 1971 earthquake the **interior** housed the two-sided triptych, with the *Blessing Christ between Mary and John*, by Francesco d'Antonio Zacchi known as Balletta (1430-1476), now in the Cathedral of San Giacomo.

Church of San Lorenzo or of the Holy Martyrs.
Above: *view of the area of the Rivellino and the basilica of San Pietro.*

On the right, towards the valley, is Largo Sette Cannelle.

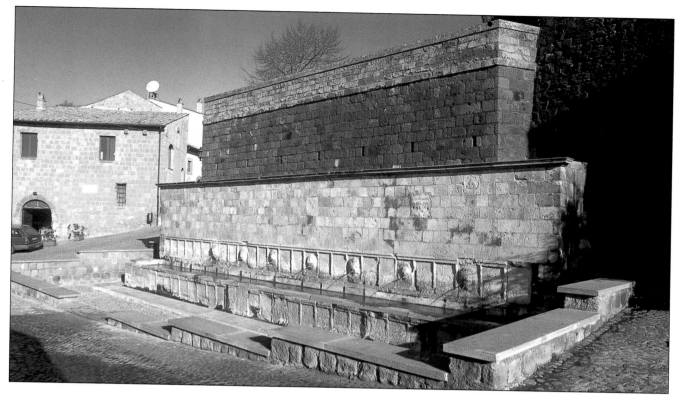

Fountain of the Sette Cannelle or of the Butinale
Largo Sette Cannelle

This is the oldest public fountain in Tuscania, and was restored in the early 14th century using Etruscan-Roman materials.

Back in Piazza Basile one can take Vicolo del Rivellino which leads to the Largo del Teatro. Further on are the remains of the ancient Via Clodia and what is left of the church of San Leonardo.

Church of San Leonardo
Via del Comune

Nothing but the facade, with a large Gothic two-light window, remains of the Romanesque-Gothic church.

The road continues and leads out of Tuscania to a fork where one road, the Strada di San Pietro, leads to the Basilica of San Pietro, and the other, the Strada di Santa Maria Maggiore, leads to this Basilica and then on to the main road.

At the fork there are the remains of Etruscan walls and the so-called Terme, or Baths, of the Regina.

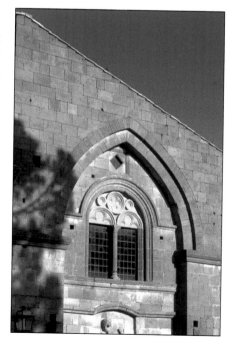

Remains of the ancient Via Clodia. Above: *fountain of the Sette Cannelle.* Right: *surviving window of the church of San Leonardo.*

Baths of the Queen (Bagno della Regina)
Strada di Santa Maria

These ruins of a Roman bathing establishment (late 1st century BC, Augustan period), at the foot of the hill of San Pietro, have traditionally been called the "baths of the Queen" [in relation to the tomb known as "Tomba della Regina" or "Tomb of the Queen", which showed a female figure, no longer visible, as if it were an ancient queen of Tuscania]. A *calidarium*, or room which served as a sort of sauna or hot baths, with a mosaic floor decorated with the figure of a dolphin, can still be identified.

Generally, as in this case, these decorations had something to do with

The so-called Bagno della Regina.

aquatic life or the use of water which flowed generously in the bathing establishments. Every Roman city, even the smaller ones, had their own bathing establishments which served

as meeting places. The villas and noble residences had their own small private bathing establishments, where guests were received or where the owners relaxed.

Sarcophagus cover in the church square of San Pietro.

Basilica of San Pietro

After the tumultuous centuries which marked the transition from the Classical period to the Middle Ages, the new symbols of religious and civic power, the basilica and the bishop's palace, were built on the height where the Etruscan acropolis once stood.

The walls of San Pietro stand on Etruscan ruins dating, at least in their early phase, to a temple of the 6th century BC in *opus quadratum*. This temple was then rebuilt several times up to the imperial Roman phase.

The facade of the church of San Pietro overlooks a grassy area between the bishop's Palace and the powerful defense towers. The path to the Basilica follows the old Etruscan route, and from the Via Clodia moves upwards along the slopes. The apse looms up ahead, rising sheer from the slope, a backdrop with decorative details which match those on the northern side of the church and visually lead the visitor on to discover the facade in its hidden scenic setting.

In the first half of the twentieth

century Pietro Toesca, one of the foremost medieval art historians of the time, dated the oldest part (apse and nave) of the church of San Pietro to the 8th century, basing himself on what little documentation there was. This was when the city became part of the Patrimony of St. Peter, after the donation by Charlemagne to Pope Hadrian I. The Basilica therefore would be a cornerstone in the history of Italian architecture, marking the transition from the building forms of the early Christian basili-

church square of the basilica.
below: decoration of the portal.

Cross section of the basilica of San Pietro (drawing by Virgilio Galati).

Apse of San Pietro. Below: *side view.*
Following page: *detail of the facade.*

ca to solutions which were to be adopted and developed after the year Thousand. It was certainly built by *"magistri comacini"* [master builders from the area of lake Como], since it differs basically from the contemporary and later monuments in Rome. It is a "mixture of crudity and inventive ingeniousness" (Toesca) with the unusually wide "dentellated" arches [similar to the ancient brackets or moldings of classical times] marching down towards the apse, so unlike the rhythms of the early

Church of San Pietro

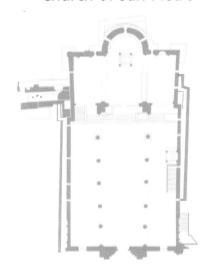

Roman basilicas. This "mixture of rudity and inventive ingeniousness" also appears in the squat proportions of the columns, in the attached half-columns on the piers just before the raised presbytery, in the row of rectangular holes on the exterior of the apse, in the arcading on both the exterior and interior of the nave. In San Pietro in Tuscania the Lombard workmen seem to have experimented with forms and proportions which were to serve as the basis for the solemn achievements of Romanesque architecture several centuries later.

Recently a different interpretation of the building vicissitudes of this unique monument have been advanced, shifting the date from the 8th to the 11th century. It would then no longer 'anticipate' the developments of Romanesque art, but could be considered the 'summa' of the universality of the Romanesque culture as such. This interpretation is based on the variety and complexity of the elements involved, and their mixed derivation, not unusual for a city such as Tuscania, located in an area of passage without natural boundaries and politically open.

In any case, between the end of the 12th and the beginning of the 13th century, perhaps after an earthquake in which part of the building collapsed, the first two bays and the present facade, marked by a great variety of influences, were built.

If the Basilica does date to the 8th century, as most art historians of the early 1900s thought, it must have been one of the most important buildings of the time in all of Italy, even though much of it was later rebuilt. According to Pietro Toesca it marked the transition from Latin to Romanesque archi-

tecture. More recently, however, according to Bonelli (1997) it is not so much an exceptional episode as it is the application of a feature that distinguished the artistic culture of central Italy from the year Thousand up to the middle of the 13th century. It was in other words a refusal to accept a vaulted construction. The patrons and builders therefore tended to continue building churches in the traditional forms, a basilica with columns, with a wooden truss roof, accepting only minor stylistic features of Lombard architecture, such as the rows of blind arcading. The basilica of San Pietro, which Bonelli thinks may date to the 10th century, a date also accepted by Galasso who compared it to examples from the Ravenna Exarcate, was renovated and enlarged repeatedly, although the distinctive features of Lombard style remained. The basic inspiration however is not north Italian and the church must be seen as an autonomous and original creation of Tuscania. All the new elements which Toesca assigned to the building on the

Close-up of the facade with the rose window.

basis of his early dating, no longer hold.

References to features of North European architecture also appear in the architecture of San Pietro (such as the 'Norman' cut of some of the voussoirs in the arches). An explanation can be found in the arrival of workmen who traveled along the pilgrim routes heading from to North to Rome and who deviated to Tuscania. It may also be however that the Norman-Swabian influences were derived from works commissioned by the Emperor Frederick II, who resided at length in the neighboring Umbria and who commissioned buildings in Terni and in Spoleto.

With respect to Toesca's conclusions, it should be noted that currently art historians are a bit less enthusiastic about the originality of this Basilica, interesting as it is.

The facade of the basilica of San Pietro.

Lion head on the facade.

one on the basilica of Santa Maria Maggiore, is a later addition to the original church plan and is the work of Umbrian marble workers with influences from Abruzzo and is not necessarily by a Roman craftsman. The splayed portal is decorated with bands of mosaic and low reliefs. Above is the rose window with concentric bands of decoration, much adorned with mosaics, while the figures of the *Evangelists* are set into the four corner sections. On either side of the rose window is a two-light opening, also with mosaic arcading, framed by rinceau motifs which encircle roundels containing demon figures on the right, and *Angels* and *Saints*, on the left. On either side of the rose window sculptured figures of *dragons chasing dog-like animals* protrude, like elongated vertical brackets. The relief with the

Winged griffin on the facade.
Below: *main portal.*

running man (half-kneeling) below the left opening has been identified as a reused piece of Etruscan sculpture.

The **facade** as it is now, marked by a large variety of influences, was rebuilt between the end of the 12th and the early 13th centuries, perhaps after collapsing in an earthquake. The solemn Cosmatesque portal in the middle of the central part is probably the work of a Roman marble worker. It is surmounted by a blind loggia above which is the great rose window between two-light openings and symbols of the Evangelists and other decorative sculptural elements. The whole is the work of an Umbrian architect, while the blind arcading along the two wings, set back from the central body, is of Pisan derivation.

According to art historians of the early 1900s, however, the central portal, like the

In the **interior,** the distinctive features of this Basilica, which for Toesca make it a fundamental in the transition from Latin to Romanesque forms, can be summed up as follows, in relation to the space and the morphology of the architectural structures: change in the relative proportions of the columns, and the spaciousness of the bays (although the intercolumniations are not identical) and the development of the double arches of which the inner one has dentil like brackets; the building of square piers instead of columns in the nave before the raised presbytery, with half-columns set against these piers as well as those of the triumphal arch (before the apse),

View of the interior.

The presbytery area.

rom which the arches spring. This association of half-columns/pier was a continuation of an architectural feature that was widely used in the Classical period, known as the concatenation of the order (and also popular in the 16th century Renaissance, with its stress on a renewal of antique structural elements). These piers are complex in plan, with a cruciform cross-section (the result of the setting together of semi-columns and semi-piers) one of the most characteristic structural features of Romanesque architecture.

The building has frequently been restored. Pope Eugene IV, for example, allocated funds for a series of works in 1443. Pope Julius II did the same thing in 1505 when he passed through Tuscania. An unusual feature before the 19th century renovations (the facade, in particular, was restored in 1870), was that the altars for the celebration of the liturgy were oriented so that the priest had to celebrate mass facing the faithful, instead of with his back to the public as was the custom before Vatican Council II. Generally it was the apse, and not the facade, which faced east. In 1841 Carlo Promis noted that in a passage from the treatise by the Sienese architect Francesco di Giorgio Martini (1439-1501: *Architettura,* *ingegneria e arte militare*, in the Cod. Magliabechiano in Florence) the author noted that "if because of the siting the temple could not face east... when it was necessary to have the altar facing west [instead of east, as was the norm], the altar should be made (so that) the priest [while looking eastwards] would be facing those present [instead of turning his back on them as was the norm]" And Promis noted that this is what happened in "three altars in the marvelous church of San Pietro fuori le mura in Toscanella". It is probable that Francesco di Giorgio was aware of this arrangement in the church of San

81

View of the crypt. Below: *detail of a capital.*

Pietro , seeing how close Tuscania was to the territories of the Sienese state and, above all, in view of the influence of Sienese art and culture on central Lazio.

Also to be noted are the Cosmati floors of the nave and the presbytery which are separated by marble transennas with 7th-8th century decorations. The marble furnishings consisting of two ciboria (the one in the right aisle is dated 1093 [a date which however seems to refer to its renovation]: the one in the presbytery has a stucco baldachin, evidently restoration) and the ambo rebuilt in the Romanesque times from early medieval elements. Etruscan sarcophagi with the deceased reclining on the lid are also set around the interior.

Before the 1971 quake the pictorial decoration of the building, originally covering the walls, converged visually on the *Ascension of Christ* in the apse conch. After the collapse of the half dome and the loss of the *Ascension*, what remains today are the subjects which framed it, such as the *Blessing Christ with a Book*, or the *Angels*, the *Apostles* and the *Divine Symbol*s. These are works of Roman School dating to the 12th century but with strong Byzantine influences, like the paintings in the right apse (with the *Blessing Christ between two Bishops*) and those in the left apse (the *Baptism of Christ* or *Stories of St. John* contemporary with those in the main apse). The frescoes of *the Life of St.*

The crypt with its columns and the reused capitals.

Peter in the upper part of the presbytery are greatly deteriorated and mostly lost (*St. Peter Healing the Lame Man*, the *Liberation of St. Peter*, the *Meeting between St. Peter and St. Paul* can still be identified). Some critics date them to the late 11th century, Italo Faldi to the first half of the 12th century. The walls of the Basilica also have fragments of the decoration that once covered the entire surface and which were lacerated by the various earthquakes which hit Tuscania throughout the centuries. In the soffits of the arches of the transept for example are a *Madonna and Child* and a *Mother of Mercy*, while on the counter-facade there is a *Crucifixion* and a depiction of *St. Bartholomew* dating to the 15th century. The church continued to be renovated with the addition of new pictorial decoration for a period of more than two hundred years.

Mention must also be made of the spacious **crypt** with nine aisles and cross vaulting supported by columns from Roman buildings. It recalls the

structure of a mosque, although no direct relationship with eastern models can be found.

The crypt seems to be later (12th century) than the initial layout of the church and made ample use of ancient columns in a variety of forms and materials, as well as Roman masonry in *opus reticulatum*. This forest of uprights offers a fine perspective effect, enhanced by the skillful groin vaulting. There is nothing comparable the other religious buildings in the city, which would seem to indicate that the earthquakes so frequent in the area destroyed vaulting of this kind which may originally have covered inner areas of the main buildings.

The frescoes in the crypt with figures of patron saints of Umbria, including *Secondianus, Marcellianus and Veranius*, date to the early 14th century. They have been attributed to the hand of Gregorio d'Arezzo, active in Santa Maria Maggiore and perhaps also in the church of San Silvestro.

Top to bottom: *Patron saints of Tuscania in the crypt and Madonna and Child with Saints in the small apse of the crypt.*

Basilica of Santa Maria Maggiore

The period to which the basilica of Santa Maria Maggiore, the old cathedral located on the slopes of the acropolis hill, belongs is highly controversial.

The traditional reconstruction of the history of the building sees it as an example of Romanesque architecture in which the syncretic qualities of the art of Tuscania shortly after 1100 come to the fore. The three portals were probably built by Umbrian marble workers with inflections of an Abruzzi style. The Lombard arcading on the sides reveals the presence of Comacine Masters, many of whom resided in the neighboring Viterbo. The small loggia over the portal displays Pisan features. This confluence of styles was further fused and amalgamated in Rome to give life to an autonomous architectural idiom. Tuscania in this period – according to the historiographic point of view advanced by Pietro Toesca in the early 1900s – was particularly aware of the various artistic styles, and an avant-

Facade of the basilica of Santa Maria Maggiore.
Left: *detail of a capital on the facade.*

gard center, giving this syncretism a unique character of its own.

According to Toesca, Santa Maria Maggiore was built in two phases around the end of the 12th century, while Noehles maintains that it dates to before San Pietro, with the exception of the central part of the facade, which was erected in the 13th century. Raspi Serra, on the other hand, suggested a date between the late 11th and the early 12th century, with subsequent changes. In any case it seems that the consecration date

View of the complex of Santa Maria Maggiore.

Above and on the right: *details of the decorations on the facade.*

of the church, October 6, 1206, can be taken as an indication that the building had been completed, with the exclusion of the decorations on the facade. The imposing truncated Romanesque bell tower across from the facade is a highly picturesque element.

Sources for the **facade** decorations are certainly varied and changes seem to have been made

more or less continuously. The decoration is disorderly and asymmetrical but lively, centered on the large rose window in the upper portion, surrounded by the symbols of the *Evangelists*; and the splendid splayed portal in the lower portion. The two are separated by a small loggia of blind arches. The sculptures on the portal reveal ties with Lombard and

Main portal.

The rose window in the facade.

St. Paul, high relief on the jamb of the entrance portal.

Abruzzo art as well as references to far-distant Auvergne models in the absolute frontality and fixed immobility of the *Madonna and Child*.

The side doors are at different levels due to the slope of the land. Over each is an oculus. The decoration of the one on the right is of classical derivation, that on the left, of Norman-Sicilian derivation.

The facade of Santa Maria Mag-

giore then is unique in its architectural and figurative decoration. In Viterbo and the neighboring towns where communities of Comacine masters had settled, Lombard influence in the churches was limited to the decoration while the plan remained that of the basilica. In Tuscania, the traditional ties with the Umbrian centers were strongly felt in the course of the renovation, and the facade adopted was typically Umbrian with a projecting central part. In the lunette of the main

portal, typically Romanesque with its stepped levels marked by small columns and with two larger columns supported by lions at either side, the iconographic theme of the *Sedes Sapientiae*, that is the *Madonna and Child* seated on a throne, as in the depictions of Solomon, symbol of Wisdom, is developed in its own way. A closer look at the ensemble reveals that this is not a real Romanesque composition, but an assembly of earlier pieces that may have been put together after one

Church of Santa Maria Maggiore

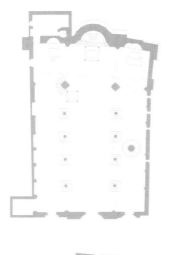

View of the interior. Left, top to bottom: *Madonna in the entrance lunette* and *decoration with monsters.*

of the many earthquakes which struck the area. Indeed the feet of the *Madonna* hang down over the lintel below, a demonstration that the figure was adapted to a place that was not in keeping with its size. The same holds for the *Lamb of God* with the lance-shaped cross on the right and *Balaam on the Ass* and the *Sacrifice of Isaac*, in the two roundels. These pieces were once certainly part of decorative friezes somewhere else. The figures on either side of the entrance door, respectively *St. Peter* on the right with his keys and a scroll; and *St. Paul* on the left (the heads were reconstructed after the origins were stolen) must also be reused material. They may have been parts of an altar since they differ in their pose. The reliefs below, deco-

View of the presbytery area.

The pulpit.
Below: *baptismal font.*

rated with rinceaux, anthropomorphic and animal figures, and perhaps Umbrian, were also certainly reused. The varying state of preservation of the individual blocks of stone seems to indicate that some were original and others were 'adapted', even using different materials (light limestones and dark nenfro. An example is the architrave). To be noted among the capitals on the left is one with the *Flight to Egypt*, while an imaginary animal referring to Hell, a *dragon*, is on the doorpost capital above St. Paul.

In the solemn **interior,** signs of work interrupted and taken up anew and renovation are clearly visible in the structures of the church. The Romanesque capitals on the columns separating the three aisles are carved with bizarre and grotesque figures. The blind arcading of the side aisles betrays Pisan and Luccan influences.

The rich marble furnishings date to various periods: the pulpit, a pastiche of reliefs dating to the 8th, 9th and 12th centuries, the baptismal font for immersion (the privilege of the baptismal font was reconfirmed by Pope Alexander II, 1159-1181), the early Gothic ciborium with frescoed vaulting, the primitive bishop's throne in the apse. The sculptures of Santa Maria Maggiore together with those on the facade and interior of San Pietro comprise one of the richest and most varied ensembles in Lazio.

According to Bonelli (1997), the church of Santa Maria Maggiore, especially in the conformation of the aisles, exemplifies the experiments which began to be undertaken in central Italy in the 8th century, even though these experiments were of a local nature, with a limited validity and not particularly innovative in concept or form. The three aisles are separated by acanthus leaf capitals (late antique and Byzantine), while Romanesque figures of *animals, demons,* and varied ornaments appear on the columns set against the piers, at the crossing. Three steps lead up to the disproportionately high presbytery and the proportions of the nave apse are at variance with those of the triumphal arch, evidence of various building phases. Attached semi-columns are to be noted on the side walls, with capitals decorated in typically Romanesque style *(processions of clerics* and animal motifs). On the left, before the crossing, is a fine pulpit in which 13th century pieces

have been assembled with others dating to the late 9th century (the figure of *St. John the Baptist* probably dates to the 13th century; it has been attributed to Guido da Como). The octagonal basin of the baptismal font in the right aisle was originally for immersion. It seems to date to the 14th century.

The frescoes with the *Apostles* in the apse are from the late 13th century and in style show they were painted by an artist from the Roman milieu with Byzantine stylistic features and harshness.

An original approach is evident in these figures when compared with what was going on in the artistic production of late 13th century Viterbo. There is an awareness of the spatial and figural conquests in the Tuscan art world, with the Umbro-Assisi production as intermediary. The tie with Rome must also have been particularly strong in Tuscania at the time these frescoes with *Apostles* were painted, since Roman 'maestranze' were called in. Many points remain to be clarified, in particular concerning the execution of these paintings and who commissioned them.

The fresco on the triumphal arch with the *Last Judgement and the patron, Secondianus*, of the early 14th century, has been attributed to Gregorio and Donato d'Arezzo, Giottesque artists whose presence in the Roman Tuscia is witnessed by works in Montefiascone, Viterbo, San Martino al Cimino, and Bracciano. They also painted the frescoes in Santa Maria Maggiore with the *Gift of the Girdle* and the *Nativity and Adoration of the Shepherds* opposite the aisles.

Various paintings in the crypt of San Pietro have been attributed to Donato alone. To be noted particularly in the *Last Judgement* in Santa Maria Maggiore is the depiction of *Hell* with the great frightening figure of the *Devil* devouring the damned, not unlike analogous images of the Etruscan Gorgon of antiquity. The remaining walls of the Basilica are rich in frescoes that can be attributed to different periods. Generally they show Saints (*St. Bartholomew* on the left wall; *St. Julian, St. Cristina* and *St. Catherine* in the left apse of the presbytery). These 14th century works are accompanied by paintings on canvas early 17th century with the *Translation of the Relics of the Holy Martyrs to Santa Maria Maggiore* (an event which took place in 1183) (on the right side of the transept), as well as scenes with *the lives of St. Jerome and St. Raymond* and the *Martyrdom of St. Cristina* in the left apse of the transept.

Fresco of the Last Judgement on the triumphal arch.

Detail in the right-hand corner.

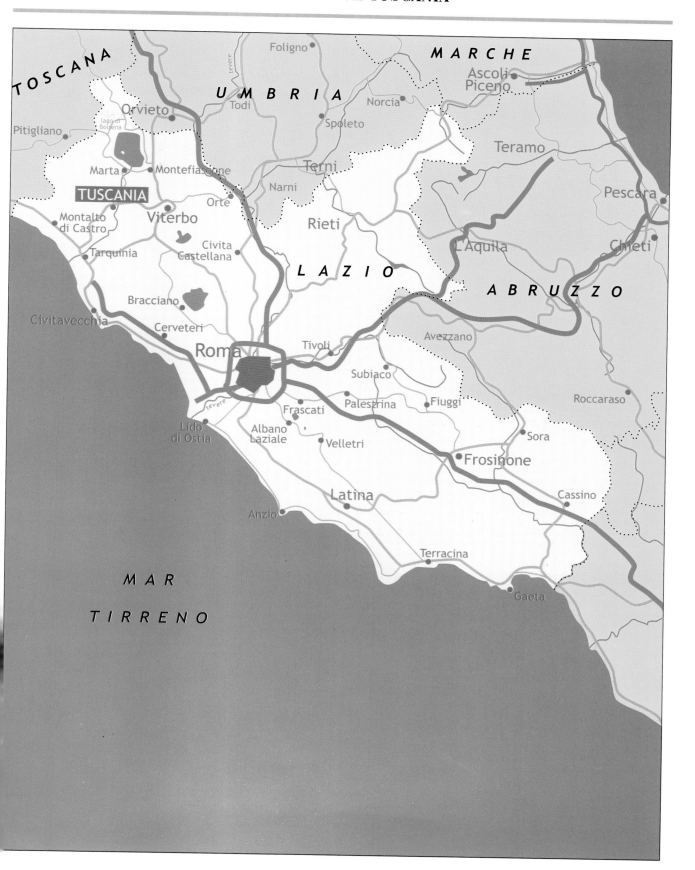

BIBLIOGRAPHICAL ORIENTATION

Historiography on Tuscania, sufficiently ample, provides a goodly amount of information on the political vicissitudes, institutions and legal systems in the city, the Etruscan remains and the monuments of medieval art which characterize it, and make it one of the most interesting towns in Central Italy.

Unfortunately the destruction of the medieval and Renaissance wall paintings and movable works of art, as well as the dispersion of the archaeological finds, furnish a picture of the city that is not as clear or as rich as it really was. There are some sectors which have interested scholars more than others, such as the problems and interpretations relating to the city's golden periods – that is antiquity and the Middle Ages – and studies and knowledge regarding the Renaissance, for example, have been neglected. This period, as well as later centuries, have left their mark on the present appearance of the city, although without the splendor of earlier periods.

The older manuscript chronicles by Giovan Francesco Giannotti (1606) and Antonio Barbacci (1704) are of a narrative or apologetic tone, while the approach of Francesco Turriozzi (1778) is more that of a historian. Even more so, in line with the times, is the work of Secondiano Campanari dating to the middle of the 19th century. He based himself on Turriozzi's studies and furnishes the fullest documentation, taken from the sources, of the city's history, even though the prose is rather pompous and it is full of the inevitable civic rhetoric.
In our days the study of Tuscania's history has been resuscitated by Giuseppe Giontella, whose research has provided detailed information on every aspect of the city through the centuries.
Archaeology, which sacked and destroyed so much in the 19th century (but which also led to the most important finds), has now become a science and is interested not in the acquisition of objects, but in increasing knowledge. Considerable progress has been made in the field of historical and artistic studies, in particular on the two major basilicas (by Campanari, Rivoira, Lavagnino, Thummler, Verder, Bruno Maria Apollonj Ghetti, Noehles, Raspi Serra) and in the field of town planning, with the exemplary study by Fusco, terminated just before the quake of 1971.

- Giannotti, G.F., *Storia della città di Tuscania* (1606), manuscript (Tuscania, Municipal Library).
- Barbacci, A., *Relazione dello stato antico e moderno della città di Toscanella e della sua chiesa* (1704), manuscript (Tuscania, Municipal Library).
- Turriozzi, F., *Memorie istoriche della città di Tuscania che ora volgarmente dicesi Toscanella*, Rome, 1778.
- Fusco, G., *Contributo alla storia di Tuscania*, in "Quaderni dell'Istituto di Progettazione della Facoltà di Architettura di Genova", November, 1971, 25 ff.
- Raspi Serra, J., *Tuscania. Cultura ed espressione artistica di un centro medievale*, Venice, 1971.
- Giontella, G., *Tuscania attraverso i secoli*, Tuscania, 1980.

Bibliographical up-date

- Promis, C., *Trattato di architettura civile e militare di Francesco di Giorgio Martini [fine sec.XV]*, Turin, 1841, 240, n 2.
- Campanari, S., *Tuscania e I suoi monumenti*, Montefiascone, Vol. I: 1885. Vol.II: 1856.
- Dennis, G. (and Ainsley), *Cities and Cemeteries of Etruria*, London, 1883.
- Pinzi, C., *Storia di Viterbo lungo il Medioevo*, Viterbo, 1887-1913, 4 vols.
- Signorelli, G., *Viterbo nella Storia della Chiesa*, Viterbo, 1940.
- Leandri, C. and Tommasi, P., *Tuscania*, Viterbo, 1962.
- Faldi, I., *Pittori viterbesi di cinque secoli*, Rome, 1970.
- *Sabato 6 febbraio 1971. Tuscania, ore 19:09* [the earthquake], Banco di Roma ed., Rome, August 1971.
- Perkins, J.W., Andrews, D., Whitehous, D., *Excavation and survey at Tuscania, 1972, a preliminary report*, "Paper of the British School in Rome", vol. XL, London, 1972.
- Perkins, J.W., Johns, J., Ward-Perkins, B., Lamarque, W., Beddoe, M., *Excavations at Tuscania, 1973, report on the finds from six selected pits*, "Paper of the British School in Rome", vol. XLI, 1973.
- Pringle, R.D., *Medieval Tower and Urban development in Central Italy: the case of Tuscania*. B.A. Diss. Southampton University, 1973; and *A group of medieval towers in Tuscania*, "Paper of the British School in Rome", vol. XLII, 1974.
- Colonna, G., *Archeologia dell'età romantica in Etruria: I Campanari di Toscanella e la tomba dei Vipinana*, "Studi Etruschi", XlI,VI, 1978 ff.
- Touring Club Italiano (with a general revision of the historical-artistic material by I. Faldi), *Tuscania*, in *Guida d'Italia. Lazio*, 1981 (4th ed.), 305-320.
- Andrews, D., *The walls of Tuscania*, 3, "British Archeological Review", International Series 125, Oxford, 1982.
- *Il Quattrocento a Viterbo*, Catalogue, Rome, 1983.
- Bravo, B., *Plinio il Giovane Epist. IX, 37, 1; l'aggettivo Tuscanus e la storia della città di Tuscania*, "Athaeneum" 1985, vol. LXIII, 508 ff.
- *Architettura etrusca nel Viterbese*, Catalogue of the Exhibition, Rome, 1986.
- Pace, V., *Pittura del Duecento e del Trecento a Roma e nel Lazio in La pittura in Italia. Il Duecento e il Trecento*, Milan, 1986, t.II, 438.
- *Tuscania [indagini archeologiche e fortuna ottocentesca]*, G. Colonna ed, Siena, 1986.
- Barker, G., Rasmussen, T., *The Tuscania project*, "Paper of the British School in Rome", vol. LVI, Hertford, 1988.
- Sgubini Moretti, A.M., *Tuscania. Il Museo Archeologico*, Rome, 1991.
- Colonna, G., *L'avventura romantica in Gli Etruschi e l'Europa*, Catalogue, Milan, 1992, 330-335.
- *I Longobardi*, Catalogue, G.C. Menis ed., Milan, 1992, 158.
- Bonelli, R., *L'architettura dal secolo VIII al XII* in Bonelli, R., Bozzoni, C., and Franchetti - Pardo, V., *Storia dell'architettura medievale. L'occidente europeo*, Rome-Bari, 1997, 128-29.
- Staccini, E., *Tuscania. La storia e i monumenti....*, Tuscania, 1998 (with an extensive bibliography).
- Pierdomenico, L.B., *Guida di Tuscania*, Grotte di Castro, n.d.

CONTENTS